Mexico

Journey of a Nation
Over a Rough
and Rambling Road

Bill Dea

ISBN 978-0-578-11786-7

Inside the Book

Timeline of Key Events

40,000 BCE - 9000 BCE: Waves of Asian migrants cross Bering Straits and populate Americas

5000 BCE: Hunters and Gatherers experiment with farming

2000 BCE-1100 CE: Rise and decline of Ancient Civilizations of Mesoamerica

1335 CE: Aztecs found city of Tenochtitlan

1519: Cortés lands on shores of the New World

1521: Aztecs defeated by Conquistadors

1521: Mexico becomes a Spanish Colony

1767: King Charles III expels Jesuits from Mexico–Mood of Mexico changes

1810: Father Hidalgo's Cry for Independence (El Grito)

1821: Independence from Spain

1822: Coronation of Emperor Iturbide

1824: Guadalupe Victoria–Mexico's first "real" president

1846-1848: Mexican-American War (U.S. seizes half of Mexico's land)

1858-1861: Reform War

1861-1867: French intervention

1910: Mexican Revolution begins

1917: Mexico adopts its present Constitution

1926-1929: Cristero War

1929: Founding of predecessor to PRI

1938: President nationalizes oil (PEMEX created)

1940: Leon Trotsky assassinated in Mexico

1981: The first Toad Suck Festival

1994: NAFTA

2000: War on Drugs–Federal troops dispatched

2012: PRI wins back presidency

Preface

Nearly 500 years ago the Conquistadors pillaged Tenochtitlan, the magnificent capital of the Aztec Empire, and made virtual slaves of its people. For the next 300 years Spain drained the colony's resources on the backs of those trapped in a cruel caste system. In 1821 Mexico freed itself from Spain, but only after a decade of bloody war. The new nation got off to a bad start when it crowned an emperor as its head of state. It should have inaugurated a president. A coup and bloodshed followed. Mexico has had presidents ever since, but some were president in name only.

After Independence many nations had eyes on making claim to Mexico. Spain, for one, had not forgotten about its former prized colony and waged war to get it back. Mexico persevered and was on its way to becoming a modern nation when, in 1846, the United States invaded Mexico and went on to grab half of its land. Within the next two decades France invaded Mexico, and there was another coup and more bloodshed before France was ousted.

Not all of Mexico's struggles were fending off foreign nations. In the mid-1800's a civil war tore Mexico apart, literally in two. Conservatives and liberals fought each other to determine the kind of government Mexicans were to live under and the place the Catholic Church was to have within that government. But the war did little other than set the stage for more adversity. The Revolution that followed in 1910 was a ten-year bloodbath followed by another religious civil war. By then Mexico had the "Banana Republic" reputation of changing presidents by assassinating them, overthrowing them, or shipping them off to another country.

The last 100 years has been a story of politicians – some good, some bad, some enlightened, and some corrupted, – but always powerful. Elections churned out presidents, governors, and mayors, many of whom left office far wealthier than they were before they took office. Drugs then came along and gave police and local officials the chance to become rich too.

Today's troubles do not stop at the Rio Grande. The United States frets about undocumented workers, border policy, drug-related crime, drugs, outsourcing of jobs, and the environment. Tomorrow something else will trigger more frenzy. In the end, each issue comes down to a referendum on Mexico.

This short book has a mission. It is to tell a well-rounded story about our neighbor to the south.

Arkansas 1995

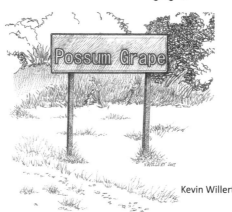

Kevin Willert

*A*sk not why we got lost on unpaved Tucker Ridge Road in the heart of Arkansas's Bible belt. I must have been distracted by a sign telling me that Possum Grape was nearby. Possum Grape is not a city. I don't think Possum Grape is a village. If it had "four corners," I don't remember them.

One web page describes Possum Grape as a "wide place on the road," another as "a populated place." It turned out to be more the former than the latter. The "wrong turn" was at a car wash just a piece up the road. (Or, was it *down* the road a piece? How would I know? I was lost.)

Our car had been plastered with road salt the day before; hence, the car wash. A brutal March blizzard had consumed much of Wisconsin and Iowa, so we were mighty happy to be on the dry roads of the greater Possum Grape area – even though we didn't know how we got there or how to get out.

The other lost occupants of our ten-year old Ford Escort were my wife, Mary, and Sara, a basset/spaniel mix. Sara was the meanest of our five dogs, thus earning the privilege of joining us rather than leaving her with the first-year high school teacher to whom we entrusted the care of our house and other four dogs for the several months we would be in Mexico.

We were on our way from our home on the frozen shores of Lake Michigan in Two Creeks, Wisconsin, to a tiny house in sunny Mexico which had a red tile roof and was tight to the curb of a cobblestone

1

street called *Angel Flores* in the lakeside village of Ajijic; all nestled in the mountains of the state of Jalisco. We bought our little *Shangri-La* just months before. It needed tons of work and we couldn't wait to get started. Maybe that is why we got lost.

Some months before the wrong turn I struck a "semi-retirement" deal with my law partners. The deal was that, having come down with a self-diagnosed bout of lawyer "burn out," I would travel one-third of each year in exchange for a one-third pay reduction. This was agreed upon in the expectation of my good partners that in time I would come to my senses. That never happened.

We really should not have been lost because we were then just about 75 miles northeast of Conway, Arkansas, which is where the Toad Suck Lock and Dam spans the Arkansas River. Everyone knows that because it was there a tavern once existed that, if still standing, which it is not, would be a shoo-in for the National Registry of Historic Places. Legend has it that it was at this tavern that boatmen would suck on the bottle "til they swell up like toads." This watering hole got even more famous after Conway started hosting the annual Toad Suck festival some thirty years ago. Well, we were not planning to go to Conway – festivities were not scheduled to start until the first weekend in May, anyway. I would like to go to "Toad Suck Daze" sometime. It sounds like three days of fun. But we were hell-bent on getting to Mexico.

We don't go to Mexico *by car* any more. Parts of Mexico have become too dangerous. But that too will change in time. (The U.S. Department of State maintains a travel advisory system that can be checked on the internet.[1]) Yet we continue to poke through Mexico's nooks and crannies as we have done for over 35 years. Our experiences are in line with those of "Mexico Mike."[2] He claims to have traveled throughout Mexico over many years without incident. He has some numbers that put the odds of being murdered in Mexico as smaller than being struck by lightning in the United States. The traveler can take this for what it may be worth – and you may want to check his blog site for updates.

The Possum Grape incident, of course, has absolutely nothing to do with Mexico. It occurred nearly twenty years ago and that was on our way *to* Mexico. It is in the early pages of this book because the rest of the book contains little that could be called "light-hearted." That is not to suggest there is a flaw in the Mexican national character – it's just that for the last 500 years, Mexicans have been battling their way out of one calamity after another. Mexico's struggles have not been laughing matters. Revolutions leave scant space for levity. It, therefore, should surprise no one that whenever Mexicans were not warring for survival, they would turn their lives inward and focus on the moment. And that is why their lives are consumed with family and friends. It is with them that they find joy and meaning. Perhaps that is what defines the Mexican ethos best.

Let the journey begin.

The Border

The U.S.-Mexico border is about 2000 miles long. It follows the Rio Grande from the Gulf of Mexico westward for about one thousand miles to a point near Ciudad Juárez. Westward from there the border is marked to the Colorado River with nineteenth-century obelisk stone monuments. The border then follows the Colorado River a short distance to another set of monuments that dots the way to the Pacific coast.

On August 18, 1971, Pat Nixon dedicated "Friendship Park" at the site of one of the monuments. The park was so named because this was the place families and friends on both sides could talk and express their love for each other. It was there a Methodist minister used to administer communion across a simple chain link fence. It was there that grandparents could see and touch their grandchildren and cousins separated by the border could swap tamales for hot dogs.

Friendship Park doesn't seem all that friendly any more. Neither does the rest of the border. In 2006 the U.S. Congress authorized the construction of about 700 miles of prison-like walls and high-tech gadgetry to be spotted at various places along the border. Visitors to

Friendship Park (up to ten at a time) must now pay admission which allows them (during restricted hours only) to peek though wire mesh openings and look at family members on the other side (touching not permitted).

The Secure Fence Act, as it is known, proved to be controversial, costly and not very secure. But it has its supporters – including those who would make the fence longer, higher, and tougher to climb over or dig under. Others think that money should be spent on more effective patrolling.

The U.S.-Mexico border is the busiest border in the world.[3] There are over forty official border crossings.[4] There are numerous twin urban centers: Brownsville-Matamoros are on the east and San Diego-Tijuana are on the west. There are many in between. These communities spread roots over a century ago as a result of foreign investment, mainly in railroads and mining. Despite images of the border-city beer joints, brothels, and gaudy souvenirs, many of the border's two thousand miles wind through spectacularly beautiful cactus-filled deserts.

The leg of our journey between San Antonio and Laredo, Texas, (our usual route) is 150 miles of flat, grassy plains bisected by U.S. Interstate 35. This rather nondescript terrain is interrupted by miles of freight trains to the east and, ahead and behind, an endless procession of cars sandwiched between eighteen-wheelers. On both sides ranch gates arch over long dusty roads that meander to sprawling homesteads far out of sight from Interstate 35.

Those "big rigs" and those long lines of freight cars are headed for, or coming from, the *"Two Laredos"* (*Laredo*, Texas, in the U.S., and *Nuevo Laredo* in the Mexican state of Tamaulipas). At just the Laredos alone, there are four international bridges and one railroad bridge. The World Trade Bridge, known as Bridge Number 4, is said to have 4,800 trucks cross each day; that is one truck every fifteen seconds.[5] This is one busy place, made more so by the explosive increase of trade since the North American Free Trade Agreement (NAFTA) became effective in 1994.

Like most border towns, the Laredos do not beckon the visitor to linger. Armed guards secure motel parking lots; they are stationed behind baggers in grocery stores; they are never far from the cash register in late night diners; they stalk around ATMs. Helicopters and predator drones patrol from the smoggy skies above.

The Laredo Chamber of Commerce would have a very different take on this, of course. And there is substance to what it would say. There are tree-lined residential areas with upscale homes, good hotels, car dealerships, strip malls, banks, plenty of good restaurants, the usual assortment of fast food franchises, and the other amenities cities offer. Business is booming in the Laredos. Still, this is not a destination place for sight-seeing vacationers. And that is just as well because much of what goes on in the Laredos and in other border towns cannot be seen anyway.

Mexican cartels smuggle some 25 to 40 billion dollars-worth of cocaine, methamphetamine, heroin, and marijuana into the United States every year – more money than comes into Mexico each year from oil, Mexico's number one legal export.[6] Most illicit drugs from Mexico are smuggled overland by truck, often concealed among legal cargo.[7] Only one in five trucks is actually unloaded and inspected,[8] otherwise commercial traffic would grind to a snail's pace.

The illegal drugs smuggled through the Laredos would hardly be a tourist attraction even if they could be seen. And, what cannot be seen in these two border cities is only a fraction of what cannot be seen elsewhere along the border – like thirty-six pounds of cocaine stuffed in the tires of a north-bound green Dodge Dakota near Niland, California – estimated value $1,100,000,[9] or the ton of marijuana discovered aboard a Freightliner truck, at mile marker 29 on Interstate 35.[10] Because it is underground, you are not going to see the 1800-foot tunnel stretching from a warehouse in Otey Mesa, California, to Tijuana, Mexico.[11] Nor will you see any of the more than one hundred other tunnels discovered in the last few decades, some of which are air-conditioned and have trolley lines up to a half mile long.[12] Unless you are a U.S. helicopter pilot patrolling the Rio Grande, you are not apt to see a rubber raft in "Smugglers Alley" in which the "hands on deck" are paddling to the north river bank to scout whether it is safe to make a "delivery."[13]

If you are sunbathing on beaches near the border you will not see smuggling in the Gulf of Mexico nor in the Pacific unless you just happen to have your binoculars pointed inches above the surface of the water – and only if you just happen to have them pointed in exactly the right place at exactly the right time. Then, on a very calm day, you might spot an SPSS protruding a few inches above the surface. As you float on your inner tube, you ask what in the world was that? According to the U.S. National Drug Intelligence Center, an SPSS is a self-propelled semisubmersible vessel used by traffickers to transport illicit drugs.[14] They typically have a four man crew. You might have a little more luck focusing your binoculars at fast boats doing end around plays. You might also catch a glimpse of a freighter or cruise ship in ·deeper waters; TCOs (Transnational Criminal Organizations) use big boats too.[15]

There is smuggling by air, but you no longer will see old Piper Cubs loaded to the eyeballs with cocaine. Most of those planes are now rusting in jungle beds or wedged to the canopies of tall mahogany trees. Drug cartels now have fleets of planes, including DC-9's.[16] These are high-flying jets, so you probably won't see them either. Then, there are ultra-light aircraft that fly too low for radar detection. [17] But, if you look just below where the ultra-lights fly, you might see four-and-one-half pound packages of marijuana soaring overhead all by themselves. It seems that some enterprising entrepreneurs were inspired by the late King Edward Longshanks of England who, in the fourteenth century, commissioned a monstrous catapulting contraption called 'War Wolf.' His Majesty thought War Wolf would be just the thing for hurling boulders at castle walls (sort of a canon without the gunpowder). Some drug smugglers from the Sonora area of Mexico must have been studying medieval warfare. They stole the King's idea and made War Wolf II to lob packages of marijuana from Mexico to the United States.[18] The border agents thought something looked out of place about this Gothic-style gadget so they filmed it and caught the geniuses who built it. King Edward, however, can rest in peace knowing that his catapult technology survived medieval times.

Not all smugglers' intentions are as thoughtful as those of the architects of War Wolf II. Some smuggling occurs unintentionally. Back in Nuevo Laredo, Andrés (not real name), a Mexican trucker, told an NPR reporter that he keeps a close watch on his truck so that no one puts a "package" in his load of blackberries.[19] Andrés does not want to take the rap for a pouch of white fluffy powder that might be slipped into his load before it makes its way up through Texas on Interstate 35. He makes sure that doesn't happen to him – but some other driver will not be that careful.

The journey of that package on someone else's truck is long, dangerous, and mysterious. It might begin on a tiny patch of bright red poppies in the terraced highlands of Colombia near the border with Ecuador. The patch is tended by a peasant farmer whom I shall call José. José never went to school so he doesn't know that 4000 years before the birth of Christ the ancient Sumerians called poppies the "flower of joy." For José, the pretty red flowers merely mean hard work, but it is work that provides food and shelter for his family. He worries that his crop may fall victim to machete-swinging squads paid for by the United States. But if his poppies survive, he will carve the sap from their pods and turn the sap into cakes; he will then put the cakes into bags. In the clandestine world of drugs José has gotten to know the shadowy broker who will come to his door and buy the cakes and then resell them to an outlaw refinery in the lowland jungle.

The refinery transforms the cakes into heroin – Dragon, or Big H, if you prefer – and the long shadowy journey from the wet jungles of Colombia has begun. The junket snakes its way through Central America and all of Mexico. Brokers along the way divide the white powder into lots, and the lots filter though a crime-infested system of distribution. It will be just a matter of time that a youngster in a high school parking lot in small-town USA will trade a fistful of cash for a brightly-colored package that is apt to ruin his life. José's labor was innocent enough. José may not think he did anything bad, but the chain of crime started with him. José does not take "joy" in thinking that.

Today's drug trafficking did not just happen. In the 1800's marijuana, opium, and cocaine were in widespread use in Mexico, mostly for medicinal purposes. Poppy and marijuana plantations were common, particularly in the northwest of Mexico. Drugs also entered Mexico from Central and South America. Once in Mexico, the next stop was the United States.

When the southern states attacked Fort Sumter the Civil War in the U.S. began, and so did the demand for morphine. Morphine (derived from opium) was used during the Civil War to alleviate pain, particularly during amputations. Many Confederate and Yankee militiamen became addicts through no fault of their own.[20] Addiction became "the Civil War disease." But drug use did not end when General Lee surrendered at Appomattox.

The U.S. was pretty casual about drug usage in the years following the Civil War. Bayer (the aspirin company) was selling heroin as a painkiller.[21] The Sears and Roebuck catalogue advertised a syringe and cocaine for $1.50.[22] That meant mail delivery. By the year 1900 there were an estimated 250,000 drug addicts in the United States.[23] Many of them were women who were led to believe that drugs were good for "women's problems."[24] Door-to-door peddlers were selling "good for what ails you" concoctions which were often loaded with morphine.

It was then just a matter of time that the dots were connected between drugs and crime. The *Journal of the American Medical Association* wrote that Negroes were becoming addicted to "cocaine sniffing."[25] Newspaper and magazine articles jumped on the bandwagon to suggest that drugs were the reason more white women were being raped.[26] The *New York Times* went so far as to suggest that cocaine made blacks shoot better.[27]

Putting a racial spin on drug use was nothing new. For years, Chinese opium dens took much of the blame for the collapse of

"American" values. A body of "anti-China" laws had found its way into the books.[28] While these laws had a lot more to do with immigration policy than drug policy, the "anti-China" laws began a long process of criminalizing drugs.

The mood of the country toward drugs heated up more by the time Teddy Roosevelt became President. Congressmen became frenzied about the "moral evils" of non-medicinal use of drugs. Teddy Roosevelt led an international effort to control opium by arranging the Shanghai Conference of 1909. In 1914 Congress passed the Harrison Narcotics Act. By 1937 morally righteous types became fixated on the evils of marijuana. Congress responded with the Marijuana Tax Act.

Cooler heads argued that the fuss in Congress was really about raising tax revenues. But, it was undeniable that the U.S. had a serious addiction problem and that something had to be done about it.

Mexico didn't see it that way. Mexico was still recovering from the Revolution of 1910 and was preoccupied with its struggling economy. Drugs were not Mexico's problem – the real problem was the demand for drugs and that problem was north of the border, not *in* Mexico. Drug trafficking had become a vital part of Mexico's economy and many in Mexico wanted a slice of it. The problem was that the Mexican drug business was not the total monopoly some longed for it to become. But better times were ahead.

The Viet Nam war and its aftermath were the times when being "beat" was in vogue and the music, poetry, and literature of the times provided a sense of legitimacy to drugs. A sellers' market mushroomed from those years and has shown no signs of letting up.

There was a period of time when drugs from Central and South America flowed through the Caribbean to south Florida without entering Mexico. But in the 1980's and 1990's Mexico's drug trade got a "shot in the arm," so to speak, as U.S. military planes and U.S. gun boats drastically slowed drug traffic along the Caribbean route. That meant that the flow of drugs from Central and South America was redirected through Mexico (the so called "balloon effect"). Needless to say, the "balloon effect" was gratefully received by those who benefited from it, mainly the cartels that claimed the rights to the vertical corridors running from one end of the country to the other. The balloon effect was one of many factors leading to today's drug war in Mexico.

Former Secretary of State Hillary Clinton described the drug war as an "insurgency."[29] The story goes something like this:

The Institutional Revolution Party (PRI) monopolized Mexican politics for the seven decades before the year 2000. Under PRI's long watch, many governors, mayors, police chiefs, and cops on the street were "on-the-take" from drug traffickers – some were involved in "hands on" dealings. The PRI turned a blind eye to the cartels – it was a "wink and nod" relationship. This changed in the year 2000 when the PRI was voted out of power and was replaced with the rival National Action Party (PAN). During the six-year presidency of Vicente Fox (2000-2006) efforts were made to rein in the drug lords, but it was not until his successor took office that the push began in earnest. In 2006 Mexico's newly elected PAN President, Felipe Calderón, dispatched some 50,000 soldiers and federal police to assault the drug cartels.

Then came headlines like these:
- **Ciudad Juárez the 'Murder Capital' of the World**
- **Children Slaughtered at Boy's Birthday Party**
- **Hand Grenade Lobbed into Guadalajara Night Club**
- **Reporter's Head Found Dangling from Bridge**
- **72 Migrants Executed in Tamaulipas**
- **Candidate for Governor Gunned Down**
- **53 Bingo Players Torched in Monterrey Casino**
- **Over 60,000 people now dead....No end in sight.**

The headlines were saying that President Calderón's war was not working. Mexicans were confused and scared as the drug cartels became ever more threatening. In 2012 the nation chose to return the presidential chair to the PRI. Now it revolves back to the PRI to see what the PRI can do.

Love them or hate them, *guns* are a fact of life – and there are a

lot of them in Mexico – but they do not come *from* Mexico. Guns are very hard to buy in Mexico. Guns can only be purchased in Mexico at an army base and strict rules tightly prescribe gun use and gun laws carry severe penalties. (There is no Mexican counterpart to the Second Amendment of the U.S. Constitution.) But just north of the border, in states such as Texas, it has been easy to buy guns, particularly at gun shows or at private sales. So it is little wonder that enterprising minds figure out how to profit from the disparity between supply and demand. About two thousand guns a day leave the United States stashed beneath the floorboards of trucks or trains, or hidden in cars going south.[30] This is the so-called "Iron River."

Here it must be said that, at the time of this writing, a frenzied national debate about "gun rights" rages in the United States as Congress and state legislators assess what may be a shifting public mood. Time will tell the outcome. But no matter how that debate plays out, it is not likely that the supply of guns in the U.S. will dry up any time soon – nor will the "Iron River."

Gun laws might well change but the appetite for guns in the U.S. knows no bounds. In Scottsdale, Arizona, a gun club offers children and their families the chance to be photographed with Santa Claus while they hold weaponry such as AK-47s and grenade launchers. Or, how about a photo of Santa flanked by a machine gun and a tripod-mounted rifle? The club manager explained it this way: *"Our customers have been looking for a fun and safe way to express their holiday spirit and passion for firearms."* [31]

Cartels need a lot of guns. They do not buy them just for shooting at *federales* or *la policía.* They are also for shooting at other cartels. Turf battles among rival cartels have made many places in Mexico a dangerous place to be.

On both sides of the border, families sit around their kitchen tables and talk about what to do about the mess created by drugs and guns. Mexicans blame the quenchless U.S. demand for drugs. They say traditional efforts to control demand – prevention, treatment, and law enforcement – have not worked. People in the U.S. blame Mexico for not controlling supply. They approve of the war on drug lords but concede that so far it has just caused more bloodshed.

Good-minded people of both countries know that blaming each other is not the answer. So they take to the streets. In May of 2011 several hundred ordinary people assembled in the streets of Cuernavaca to march into the center of neighboring Mexico City to protest the government's failure to address crime and violence.[32] In August of 2012 one hundred people, led by Mexican poet Javier Sicilia, traveled from San Diego to Washington D.C. in a "Caravan for Peace" to protest American drug policies.[33] But what can either government do? Mexico may continue its crackdown, beef it up, tweak it, look the other way, or try something new and different. Mexico will have to decide what it will do. In the U.S. several solutions are tossed around.

Some argue for *decriminalizing* the use of drugs. Decriminalization is different from *legalization* – under decriminalization *production* and *distribution* continue to be criminal acts that carry severe penalties, but the penalty for *usage* is more like getting a traffic ticket. The notion is that punishing users is different from punishing robbers or murderers because users have not violated the rights of others; therefore treat the use of drugs as a health issue and redirect the money spent on punishing users to getting at production and distribution. Look at The Netherlands where one can buy marijuana in "coffee houses;" still the Dutch have one of the lowest rates of marijuana use in Europe.[34] The question posed by decriminalization is whether the U.S. public would ever be persuaded to vote that way. So far, it has even been reluctant to vote for the non-medical use of marijuana. At the time of this writing, nonmedical possession of small amounts of marijuana has been decriminalized in only a slim minority of states. And, marijuana is illegal federally.

Some believe the U.S. should *regulate* drugs, like we regulate alcohol. The theory is that it is the underground nature of drugs that makes controlling them difficult. Get it out in the open and then regulate use. But look what alcohol has done to our national health, crime rate, divorce rate; consider the destroyed lives, lost jobs, traffic deaths, and overcrowded prisons. Skeptics ask: Would not "regulated" drugs result in even greater social costs?

Others suggest the solution is to tinker with *enforcement* options, like deploying available (and limited) enforcement resources against just the biggest offenders. Maybe harpooning the biggest fish will deter smaller fish and will cause fish just learning to swim to swim straight. Who knows? Maybe state troopers should randomly test folks at road blocks just like they test motorists for alcohol. Maybe have parole officers and police randomly test ex-cons.

Some people think the answer lies in *prevention* – more drug education in the schools, in the streets, and in the prisons.

In the long run, maybe the best that can be done on either side of the border is "a little bit of this and a little bit of that." And, hope for the best. There could be reason for cautious optimism. On the supply side, just maybe, succeeding generations of cartel families will tire of living on the lam, choose to pursue higher education, and go "legit." They know that not everyone south of the border is a drug lord or a lackey of one. Maybe they long to be neither. On the demand side, remember that not all places north of the border are drug infested. The vast majority of U.S. citizens were never "into" drugs, know next to nothing about them, are afraid of drugs, and want nothing to do with them. One would think that common sense might prevail in time.

Seeing that we still are at the border it may be time for a detour. Who has ever taken a road trip without one? Let's take one now. I will end this account about the border by telling you something about the

border that you may not know: It is not where it used to be.

Until 1848 Mexico's (and earlier, Spain's) notion of the border included all of what are now Texas, California, Utah, Colorado, Wyoming, Nevada, and New Mexico. The problem was that, because Mexico's population was then centered so far to the south, there was no way for Mexico to secure this far-reaching territorial claim. To stave off incursions from Indians and the Texas Rangers and ultimately the United States, Mexican citizens (Catholics only) were enticed by land grants to settle north of the Rio Grande. Protestants did not need to apply.

The flow of Mexicans north of the Rio Grande clashed with our "Manifest Destiny," being a mixed bag of imperialistic notions coupled with an obsession to lead the world toward liberty and democracy. We were the biblical "shining city on a hill."

The ensuing Mexican-American War (1846-1848), begun by President Polk on grounds reminiscent of the WMD delusion, forced Mexico to pull back the border to its present location along the Rio Grande, thus adding about one-third to the land mass of the United States. And so it was that, at the cost and humiliation of losing the war, Mexico's border problem was brought to a swift and, for Mexico, an adverse conclusion. That was not quite the end of it, however. Surveyors later discovered that the Treaty of Guadalupe-Hidalgo had some mapping mistakes, most notably leaving off a chunk of southern Arizona and New Mexico that U.S railroad barons had their eyes on. But that was all fixed by the Gadsden Purchase a few years later – yet another bad deal if you were a Mexican.

I am not proposing giving Texas (or the other states) back to Mexico. However, I am not the only one who ever thought of it. In 1917 Germany sent a coded telegram intended to reach high levels of the Mexican government. The substance of the telegram was that Germany would help Mexico restore the land Mexico lost to the United States if Mexico would connive with Germany in its World War I effort. The Brits, however, intercepted the telegram and decoded it – so Mexico never had the opportunity to officially decline the German offer.[35] It was just as well because by then Mexico had no desire to wage war with the United States. That made a lot of Texans happy.

South of the Border

*I*t's one thing to drive to the border and it is another to get to the other side of it. First, your car will need a permit. Mexico has very unforgiving laws requiring cars brought into Mexico be registered with the authorities and that permits be affixed to the windshield at all times. A permit is to a car what a visa is to a tourist. Getting a permit (at least getting one in Nuevo Laredo) was a stand-in-this-line-and-then-in-that-line process that put you, your car, and your credit card into Mexico's vast data base. Now it can be done online. Either way, the end result is posting a bond with a credit card. The bond is charged to your account immediately, but is refunded if you leave the country with the same car you drove into the country. Common sense suggests that you "unregister" when you exit the country; otherwise, when you get home you will see hefty charges remaining on your Visa bill.

The system does work, however. An organization that ranks the countries of the world in terms of "ease of doing business" gives Mexico what appears to be an "okay-to-good" rating.[36] I would give the permit process the same rating. But getting the permit is not the end of dealing with border officials.

You are not really *in* Mexico, however, until you cross a checkpoint 26 kilometers south of Nuevo Laredo. If you are very lucky you might get waived through. If you are very unlucky you might be subject to an investigation of all the car's contents, the car itself, and an item-by-item analysis of everything in the roof top carrier. A snarling dog in the backseat may speed the inspection along, but don't count on it; they have dogs too.

Once the border formalities are behind you, your Mexican adventure can begin. This is a country that is very different than the United States. It has been that way from the beginning. The natives who occupied the grand and ancient civilizations that once prospered south of today's border were nothing like the natives who roamed the forests and plains north of it. They shared one thing in common, however – they were each to be invaded by strangers. In 1519 a controversial adventurer from Castile by the name of Hernán Cortés landed on Moctezuma's shores. Two years later a Spanish monarchy would begin a 300-year reign over the land we now call Mexico. Some 2000 miles to the northeast – and just 60 plus years later – an English aristocrat by the name of Sir Walter Raleigh explored the land that was to be the colony of Virginia. Soon thereafter England's Queen Elizabeth I would lay claim to the colonies that would blossom into the United States. Historical events leading to independence from these very different mother countries would be on unrelated trajectories. Two separate nations would emerge from colonial status with distinct cultures and separate identities. And remember too that Mexico, unlike the United States, had earlier been home to the great civilizations of the Olmecs, Mayans, Aztecs, and others. No wonder the two countries have vastly different sights, sounds, and smells. And no wonder Mexico City is so different from Washington D.C.

So, say adios to the familiar. Ahead lie sunbaked deserts, cacti and distant snow-capped mountains; the car radio rattles off commercials in Spanish; the only gas you can buy is state-owned PEMEX; even the roadside *hamburguesas* and *papas fritas* don't taste like the hamburgers and French fries you left behind. It is hard to imagine how one can enter such a different culture by crossing just one border. You are in Mexico – make no mistake about it.

If the factory in your home town "moved to Mexico," it probably went the way of a *maquiladora*. The border area is well known for *maquiladoras.* These are Mexico's sweat shops, a/k/a "assembly plants." They are all over the place, even though they used to be mostly along the border.

Were it not for the dismal reality of *maquiladoras,* the word itself has a nice enough ring to it. *Maquiladora* sounds something like a rum and fruit cocktail that might be served poolside in a hollow coconut. But forget about putting a nice spin on the word. *Maquiladora* has nothing to do with mixed drinks. The derivation of the word goes back to Old Spain. A *maquila* was the portion of grain a miller charged for processing other people's grain. In other words, if I were a farmer in Old Spain, it would cost me a *maquila* (a portion of my grain) to have a miller mill my grain.

The concept is simple; it is to delegate an aspect of production to someone with the capacity to perform that function either more efficiently or for less money. So it is that foreign manufacturers look to *maquiladora* workers to convert foreign parts to finished products.

The *maquiladora* program began in the 1960s. The idea behind the program was to allow foreign investment in Mexico in the form of assembly plants equipped with the foreigner's equipment and controlled by the foreigner's managers, but using Mexico's labor. For example, under the program a U.S. company is allowed to import material and equipment into Mexico on a duty-free and tariff-free basis for assembly under that company's supervision and then export the assembled products back to the United States to be sold there or elsewhere. Maquiladora products can also be sold in Mexico. In other words, the *maquiladora* that displaced your home town factory is making the same products it used to make but it is doing so in Mexican assembly plants using Mexican workers.

Today there are some 3000 of these sweatshops owned by companies from the U.S., Japan, Europe, and elsewhere.[37] They employ some one million Mexican workers,[38] mostly women, who assemble electronic devices, sew garments, and put together sundry other items to be gobbled up by consumers world-wide at bargain basement prices.

Wages are pathetic (as low as 50 cents an hour for unskilled; $1-$2 for skilled workers).[39] Labor abuses are common. Some workers log 75 hours a week.[40] Most live in dismal shanties, some without electricity. Many of the workers come from the rural southern part of Mexico only to find out that their cost of living is higher than it was back home. If work under these conditions is not bad enough, some workers are laid off because their *maquiladora* moved to Asia where labor is even cheaper.

There are other problems such as waste management, environmental concerns, crime, and human rights abuses (especially to women).These conditions have caused protest from activist groups throughout the world. England's rock band *Radiohead* has a song decrying the *maquiladora* situation.

It is not easy to put a good spin on *maquiladoras* except to say that the program does provide work to those who are desperate for work. And, in a world of economic disparity where many people are struggling, maybe it is good that affordable *maquiladora*-made garments and gadgets are on store shelves despite the social and moral costs. Then too some will contend that *maquiladoras*, by providing low-cost production south of the border, free up capital for expanding U.S. operations north of the border.[41] Arguably there is a synergistic relationship that benefits both countries. Lastly, some companies, like G.E., are bringing some "outsourced" manufacturing back home.[42] Others are said to be looking at "reshoring" too.

On that upbeat note, let us look at the brighter side of Mexico.

Once in Mexico, we usually spent the first night at Concepción del Oro, a town in north-central Mexico about mid- point in a fourteen hour drive from the border to our destination in central Mexico. I assume from the name "Oro" (which translates into "gold"), that gold was discovered there. Today this is an agricultural community of about 11,000 inhabitants. It is nestled in a sun-drenched high desert valley surrounded by the Sierra Madre Mountains. In addition to beans, corn, and oats in the farm fields, the surrounding desert has a lot of cacti. A roadside restaurant serves as the local bus stop. And, there is a pet-friendly motel connected to the restaurant. Although modest, this place always was a welcoming oasis after driving hours on lonely desert roads. The lady behind the desk didn't stop us from unloading our dogs, but my guess is that she must have at least thought about it. (Dog lovers, take note: after our first trip, we took *all* our dogs to Mexico.)

Cricket, the Newfoundland, was by far our biggest dog and was usually the first to want to stretch out after long hours in a cramped car. She seemed terribly out of place sniffing cacti outside of our motel window. The other dogs preferred the cool tile floor.

As the sun began to set behind the mountains, I began to set up my bar. This involved a jug of Mexican gin, quinine water, crumpled crackers and a wedge of cheese from Wisconsin, all neatly arranged on a table removed from our room and placed outside our door. There we could gaze at the sunset while trying to ignore the trucks roaring past on the too-close highway.

The sight of the gin and cheese quickly attracted a married couple from a nearby unit – and, split seconds later, a few of their buddies bellied up to my bar as well. I didn't know we were hosting a reception, especially on an international scale, but it quickly became just that. It turned out that our uninvited guests were from The Netherlands. We never thought of this motel as a place travelers spent more than one night. Wrong again – our newly found friends from Holland stayed there for days on end. They stayed a long time at our party, too.

Hans and Gerta and their friends didn't bring any liquor, but they did bring empty glasses from their rooms and they brought along a stack of photographs that must have been three inches thick. After they loosened up with a bit of my gin, they treated Mary and me to an unabridged lecture on the many species of cactus they photographed while trekking the environs of Concepcion del Oro.

One might guess that Dutchmen were more inclined to favor tulips. Not these folks. As though they were leaking classified information, they divulged to us that the desert surrounding Concepción del Oro is to cactus what Holland is to tulips. I kept thinking they may break the monotony with an occasional snap shot of a beautiful young maiden in wooden shoes. Forget the wishful thinking; these Hollanders were on a cactus-only mission.

Just about then a fleet of white pick-up trucks maneuvered into parking places in front of neighboring rooms. It turned out that the occupants were long-term motel guests too. They were U.S. employees returning from a hard day's work in the hot desert searching for precious metals the Colonists neglected to loot. They didn't stick around for cocktails. Their minds were set on showering and going out for beer. Maybe it was the stack of pictures that scared them away.

The next morning we were on our way again. There was a lot of desert ahead. I kept thinking about those cactus-obsessed Dutchmen. And then, I started thinking why others go to Mexico.

Not many folks come to Mexico exactly as did Jerónimo de Aguilar; nor did many foreigners get there before Aguilar got there. In fact, Aguilar got there before Cortés got there – in 1511, to be exact.[43] Aguilar was a Spanish Franciscan friar who had the misfortune of being shipwrecked off the coast of Yúcatan while en route from Pánama to Santa Domingo. He and several companions jumped on a life boat and landed on the beaches of the modern-day state of Quintana Roo. Their welcoming party turned out to be some very hostile natives who decided to sacrifice the uninvited strangers to the Maya gods. One might say that tourism in Quintana Roo got off to a bad start. But there is more to this true story, so gather around.

Aguilar and a fellow survivor, Gonzalo Guerrero, managed to escape deep into the interior where they were greeted, this time, by friendly Mayan Indians. Guerrero fell right into Mayan life. He loved it. He became a war chief, married a rich Mayan woman and the happy couple had two lovely children. When Chief Xamanzana realized that Aguilar was not adjusting as well as Guerrero, the Chief offered Aguilar some young maidens to bolster his spirits. But Aguilar stuck to his vow of celibacy and declined the offer. Xamanzana was dumbfounded. He also was quick to spot the perfect candidate for an open staff position; he put Aguilar in charge of making sure that the Chief's harem didn't mess around with anyone other than the Chief.

There is more: In 1519 Cortés heard about Aguilar and Guerrero and wanted to meet them in the worst kind of way. For one thing, they had

21

learned the native language, which Cortés rightly assumed could work to his advantage. How could he persuade natives to join ranks with him if he couldn't talk to them? Cortés finally did manage to meet up with Aguilar. (Actually, they would have missed connecting with each other but for Aguilar paddling a canoe out to sea to intercept Cortés's boat. It's a good thing he did because Aguilar went on to be a translator for Cortés during the Spanish Conquest.) The two must have hit it off well because a few years after the Conquest Aguilar built a three story mansion very near Cortés' palace. No poverty vow for this friar! Aguilar's gracious residence later became the home of the first printing press in the New World. Today it is a bookstore.

The story of Aguilar and Guerrero may seem bizarre, but you now know why at least two people went to Mexico – other than Hans and Gerta, that is. So this story ends.

Hans and Gerta probably could best be described as amateur botanists from Europe. But there was another botanist from Europe who got to Mexico about two hundred years before Hans and Gerta got there. His name was Baron Alexander von Humboldt whom Charles Darwin described as "the greatest scientific traveler who ever lived." The Baron's findings and descriptions of Mexico (and many parts of Latin America) so impressed the Mexican government that he was offered a position in the Mexican cabinet, but he refused. The Baron had other things on his mind, like exploring Siberia and writing *Kosmos,* an attempt to unify all science into a multi-volume set of books. He also had an invitation to spend some time with Thomas Jefferson. With friends like that, he probably would have sent his regrets to my cocktail party in Concepción del Oro.

Unlike Aguilar and Guerrero, the Baron, and Hans and Gerta traveled to Mexico on purpose. We go there on purpose. And, there are others who travel to Mexico on purpose. There are the sun bathers, golfers, snorkelers, deep sea fishermen; conventioneers; those who explore the Colonial cities, museums, art galleries and ancient ruins; agenda types (save the rain forests, human rights activists, etc.); college kids and the surfing set; backpackers; aging beatniks; artists and authors. The simple fact is that a lot of people go to Mexico, and they keep going back. Despite headline news about drug cartels, swine flu, and its fabled drinking water, Mexico is one of the most visited countries in the world with over 20 million tourists a year.[44]

Expatriates – there are a lot of them. The prospect of a fresh start or a new adventure tugs away at most of us. Over one million U.S. citizens reside in Mexico.[45] Why so many? In the little village of Ajijic (to which we are headed) there is a saying that might offer an explanation, were it accurate – but it is not. The expression is: *"Everyone here is running away from something,"* typically a reference to baggage from a bad marriage, a lost job, high cost of living, severe winters – you name it. I never liked that expression because it is flat wrong. We have many happy and well-adjusted expatriate friends who chose to fill out their years in this sunny country they have grown to love. They were faced with the choice that sooner or later faces most everyone: cling to an unsustainable life style or try something new. Expatriates opted for the latter. It may not be perfect. Children and grandchildren do not live next store, Medicare doesn't apply, and the language is different – but they are surrounded with spirited people with a world view. While we are not expatriates, we have observed them in Mexico and they seem to be active in their communities and they certainly appear to be having fun. Of course, there are exceptions. Admittedly, there are those who become disillusioned and return to their native home.

Then there are a few who might like to be back home but have compelling reasons not to. Take the case of an attorney who moved to Mexico after the heat got too hot in the kitchen back in Tennessee. In 1999, or about then, my wife and I became aware of a trendy coffee and pastry shop about six blocks from our house in Ajijic. We stopped there one night and were seated by the owner. I told him how glad I was that we found his place. So was the TV series *60 Minutes.* Soon rumors were swirling around our little village of a murdered wife in Tennessee, her body being rolled in a carpet, abducted children, extradition proceedings and enough other intrigue to keep our village spellbound for months. Anyone wanting to follow up on this story can read what pops up on Google. Just punch in the name Perry March.

Well, so much for pondering why people go to Mexico. We drive on.

I have had a number of traffic infractions in Mexico. The bad news for drivers with foreign licenses plates is that they will be held to a stricter standard than that which applies to vehicles with Mexican plates – or with no plates at all. That is putting it as delicately as possible. The good news is that if you do get "pulled over," not everything is necessarily lost.

A helmeted motorcycle policeman, with aviator sun glasses and high black boots, pulled me over one day while we were breezing through a city in central Mexico we had never before visited. Mary, who speaks much better Spanish than I speak, served as interpreter from the right front seat while Sara, in the back seat, upheld her reputation as the "mean one" by snarling non-stop at the policeman.

While the officer compared my face with the photo ID on my driver's license, he let it be known that I could have my license back on Tuesday after the Judge set the fine and I paid it. I reminded the good officer that Tuesday was three days away and that my wife and dog would like to get on their way – and so would I. That didn't move him a bit. I tried a different approach. "Officer, I have an idea. Why don't I give you some pesos and you pay the fine for me next Tuesday?" I could see in a flash that this was a sensible cop – except for one thing: He said *he had no receipts.* He had just uttered the magic words! We both then knew that a deal without a paper trail was in the making. It was just a matter of *how much?*

I threw out my opening offer. He insisted that the judge would want more. I countered that the judge would be in a forgiving mood after the long holiday weekend. The bickering continued. When I got the officer down to the pesos I had with me (less enough to get to the next ATM) this roadside incident was resolved *without* a receipt .In fact, it got so amicably resolved that this nice young man gave us a motorcycle escort to the highway I had zoomed past just before he stopped me. With a red flashing dome light rotating high over his handlebars, he cheerily waived us good bye. Sara curled up in the back seat and went back to sleep.

A word to the wise: Mexico is said to be cracking down on this sort of thing.

"The Bite"

The bite (*la mordida*) has nothing to do with a dog bite. It is the traditional way of getting things done in Mexico. Once again, look to world-wide rankings. Transparency International gives Mexico a corruption perception rating of 100 on an index of 182.[46] To put this in perspective, New Zealand is number 1(least corrupt); the United States has a ranking of 24. At least both Mexico and the United States are better rated than last place Somalia.

The usual explanation for police corruption is that police are drastically underpaid and need *la mordida* to make ends meet. Many Mexican police officers still earn $350 per month or less, despite efforts to increase wages in the fight against corruption.[47] The same case is made in behalf of public workers generally, namely that "the bite" is just a part of their compensation package.

El que no transa no avanca ("He who doesn't sell out, doesn't get ahead.") This rationalizing may be the public mood but hardly is in the best interests of Mexico, and it results in big money. According to one report, 9% of Mexico's GDP gets siphoned off to corruption – more than is spent on education and defense combined.[48]

Another explanation of the bite is that it has historical roots going back to the days of Cortés. The Spanish Crown handed out government positions in New Spain from the Viceroys on down. These were not always made based on merit – the appointee paid for the honor of being chosen. The King could hardly be shocked to discover that his appointee would seek to recoup the fee paid to the Crown. And what better source could there be than the minions the appointee was to hire? Thus was the start of trickle down corruption.

The King's hiring practices were not unique. The Church followed suit with appointments of bishops, priests and other clergymen. A strain of "the bite" then spread relentlessly to politics and business. A 2005 report by the Center for Economic Studies of Private Sector in Mexico City found that one out of five businesses admitted to making "extra official" payments to win public contracts, speed government paperwork, or skirt regulations.[49] An article about Walmart's Mexico subsidiary, Wal-Mart de Mexico, was splashed in the *New York Times* claiming that millions of dollars of bribes were behind Wal-Mart's explosive rate of growth in the early part of the last decade.[50]

La mordida has become baked into Mexico's culture. So, let's not be too hard on the policeman who led us out of town – or, for that matter, on me or Walmart.

Destination

Lake Chapala

*W*e were headed for the village of Ajijic on the northern shore of Lake Chapala. The Indian spelling is *Axixic*. In the native tongue Axixic means "the place where the water bubbles up" (hot water springs). Lake Chapala is Mexico's biggest lake, located about 45 minutes south of Guadalajara. The area between the cities of Chapala and Jocotepec (see map following) is today called *La Ribiera*, but is referred to locally as *The Lakeside*.

Lake Chapala
(Laguna de Chapala)

Guadalajara
(45 Minutes by car)

Chapala (City)
Ajijic

Mezcala Island
(Presidio Island)

Lake Chapala

Jocotepec

The first humans to discover this fresh water lake in the mountains must have been surprised to find a lake there at all; and they must have been even more surprised when they found out how big it was. The lake is about 50 miles long (from east to west) and about 12 miles wide (from north to south). In the 12th century Nahuatl Indians took notice that the lake was swarming with whitefish, the sky above it was alive with pelicans, and flora was everywhere – so it was no surprise they settled there. But the Spanish Conquest of 1521 meant the end of the Indians having the lake to themselves. Then the monks arrived charged with the mission of converting the natives of the lake communities to Christianity. The friaries they built became the nuclei of the villages that today line the lake's north shore in a narrow band between the water's edge and the wooded mountains. The first such mission was established in Jocotepec in 1529, then in Ajijic in 1531, and by 1548 Chapala had a missionary.

Life in the villages along the lake was pretty tranquil for nearly 300 years as the fishermen fished, the farmers farmed, and the clergy prayed and administered to the villagers' needs. That was to change on September 16, 1810, when, 217 kilometers away, a priest named Hidalgo shouted his famous Cry for Independence. The story of Mexico's Independence from Spain is set forth in Chapter 14, but a part of that story occurred at Lake Chapala. There a small group of fishermen and farmers gathered to rally for the cause of Independence. The Spanish responded with a vengeance. They sent men, weapons, and supplies to the lake. They even hauled boats overland to wage the war at "sea." To ward off the Spanish assault, a fisherman named José Encarnación Rosas and a villager from Mezcala named José Santa Ana set up a fortress on a tiny island in Lake Chapala. From that little island the vastly outnumbered rebels held off the Spanish from 1812 to 1816. A priest named Castellanos Mendoza, who was born in the area, returned to Lake Chapala to join the fight. This was hardly the war that would lead to Independence, but it mattered a lot to the people who lived along the lake. Not much came out of it except the Spanish were humiliated and the rebels were able to surrender without being punished. The isolated little island, later named Presidio Island, became the site of a prison for a while. Folks can now visit the island by paying an off-duty fisherman for the 20 minute boat ride and explore ruins. A causeway now spans the lake there.

For centuries *The Lakeside* was sheltered from tourism mostly because it was hard to get to it. Four hundred years ago the horseback ride from Guadalajara to Chapala took two days over bandit-infested dusty trails.

By the mid-1800s travel time was shortened with stagecoaches, but stagecoaches took twelve hours and a change of horses. As the years rolled by a dirt road made it possible to go from Guadalajara to Chapala in four or five hours. (The trip today takes about 45 minutes). And so, *The Lakeside* proved to be a difficult place for tourists to ruin. However, entrepreneurial minds were dreaming up how to ruin it another way – by linking Lake Chapala via a commercial water route to Guadalajara. In the early 1830's the idea of canalizing the River Santiago was bantered around. In the mid-1800's some Frenchmen tinkered with a variation of the same idea but they lost their enthusiasm for the project when faced with the impracticalities of it – or perhaps they lost their nerve when Maximilian I (who briefly served as the France-appointed emperor of Mexico) was sent to the firing squad. Either way, the idea was shelved. But others saw potential for steamships to ferry passengers and cargo to and from the villages that lined the lake. In 1868 the steamer *Libertad* was launched. Historian and travel writer Tony Burton says the *Libertad* (described by one passenger as a "wonderful old tub") toppled over in 1892 drowning most of its two-hundred (plus) passengers.[51] The loss of the *Libertad* did not spell the end of boats steaming on Chapala's waters, however. The two-tiered passenger boat *El Viking* and the freighter *Tapatio* (among others) continued to finesse their way around fishermen and sailboats as they steamed to and from village ports. But the steamboat years started to fade shortly after the turn of the century to be replaced by rail and hard surfaced roads.

It was during this time that the quiet Indian fishing villages on Lake Chapala were discovered by elite vacationers from Europe and elsewhere, including Mexico's upper crust. It was there that Pofirio Díaz, Mexico's long term dictator, often relaxed on weekends with Mexico's high society at "The Mango Grove," the mansion of his brother-in-law whom people called "El Chato." Alberto Braniff, of aviation fame, built a stately mansion in Chapala. (It is now a restaurant.) A wealthy Norwegian from Kristianund named Christian Shejetnan became so captivated by the lake that he settled along its shores in 1908 harboring grand plans for the area, including a yacht club (which he built) and a ritzy hotel (which he did not build). Shejetnan went on to founding a rail line that provided velvet-chair service daily to well-healed vacationers headed for *The Lakeside*. Thanks to Shejetnan (and the government permitting a rail extension connecting Chapala to the national rail system), moneyed folks could then leave Mexico City or Guadalajara by train and arrive at Chapala's depot in the comfort of gleaming red coaches. Shejetnan's train service began April 20, 1920, and the last train chugged away from Chapala's depot just before the line went bust in 1926. The railroad station in Chapala stands to this day.

This elegant old building was the masterpiece of Shejetnan's good friend, Guillermo de Alba, a renowned area architect who had studied architecture in Chicago. The station has now been revitalized as a museum and cultural center.

Chapala's Train Depot
© Enrique Velázquez / Lic.courtesy of Belva y Enrique Velázquez Studio, Ajijic • www.mymexicoart.com

In time, the well-to-do went on to other watering holes. Artists, authors, playwrights and movie stars took up the slack. Tennessee Williams wrote *The Poker Night* in Ajijic. The book later became *The Street Car Named Desire*. D. H. Lawrence worked on *The Plumed Serpent* while biding time in Chapala.

The 50's and 60's brought some of the beatnik crowd to *The Lakeside*. Their presence was soon overshadowed by a wave of retirees and snow birds from Canada, the U.S., and Europe in search of sun, bridge, tennis, and affordable living. *The Lakeside* also proved to be a refuge for remarried retirees who wanted a little distance from the "baggage" of prior marriages.

Whatever their reason for being at *The Lakeside*, it is a beautiful area with upscale homes, restaurants, and shops. However, the overall tenor of *The Lakeside* is decidedly Mexican, notwithstanding the invasions from outside. *The Lakeside* claims to have the second best climate in the world. Someplace in South Africa is reputed to have a better climate, but don't try telling that to anyone living in *The Lakeside*. Homes have neither furnaces nor air conditioners, although many have wood burning fireplaces. The summer months of "rainy season" create a semi-tropical climate where purple jacaranda trees and yellow and pink primavera trees flourish.

In the summer of 1994 Mary and I visited the area in hopes of finding a rental for the ensuing winter months. At that time there was little available. We did, however, stumble upon a neglected house located in Ajijic on a dusty cobblestone street filled with small children, dogs, and decommissioned cars in various stages of recovery. The one-story house was the color of road dirt and its front butted up to the narrow street it faced. The exterior walls on both sides were shared with the neighbors' homes. It had a red clay tiled roof on which was perched a black *tinaco* (water tank) to provide running water for the hours each day that village water was shut off. The interior of the tiny house had exposed timber beams. The walled garden was overgrown and neglected. Never mind that the kitchen was miniscule, that the one toilet barely flushed, and that exposed electrical wires were tacked to the inside walls. With it all, the place was screaming with charm (no doubt owing to the fact that it had been owned by an architect/designer on two prior occasions).The neighborhood was just what we wanted. It was love at first sight.

The bad news was that the house was not for rent, although it was for sale. The good news was that the asking price approximated the cost of a better-than-average new car. Having no intention at the time of buying, we returned to our hotel for a nap. Unable to sleep, I slipped away and found a pay phone in the town square to call my bank back home. I wanted to know if my banker would finance my fantasy or would think I was delusional. The response was not enthusiastic. It ended with a qualified loan approval and an understanding that the paperwork could wait until I got back home. I scurried back to the hotel to get Mary's okay and within minutes I made a low ball offer of purchase through the owner's agent. The offer was rejected within minutes and with no counter offer. Feeling greatly relieved, we spent that evening thinking we had ducked a dangerous bullet.

The sun was rising the next morning as we taxied to the airport for our flight back home. Feeling rejuvenated and emboldened, I suggested to Mary that, while I was checking in the baggage, she call the broker and raise the offer by $5000.She tried, but true to the reputation of Mexican pay phones at the time, her repetitive attempts did not go through. So it was that we flew home having ducked yet another bullet.

The following day I returned to my law office. On top of the usual assortment of accumulated stuff lawyers deal in, was a fax from the broker congratulating me on having just bought a house! It seems the seller had second thoughts and decided to accept my low-ball offer after all. Every law student learns in Contracts 101 that when an offer is rejected the offer is automatically withdrawn. That didn't bother the broker. So it was that we firmed the deal up without the extra $5000.

Our Mexico House
Guarded by Daffy, Sara (the "Mean One") and Sam

While on the subject of real estate deals in Mexico, I have to mention that a few years later I bought a lot on which to build a garage. The only problem was that the lot was several hundred feet from our house with several other houses in between. And did I fail to mention that the lot was on the other side of the street? The lot was owned by Lorenzo, a kind and good old man who had made a living fishing on Lake Chapala. Lorenzo, however, never grasped the nuances of dealing in real estate. Nonetheless we verbally agreed on price, and I had a broker prepare the paperwork.

Here you may be interested in learning something of buying real estate in Mexico. Being a lawyer didn't help me a bit. Mexico has its own rules. Back then a foreign buyer had to put ownership in a Mexican bank trust (*fideicomiso*) which, so far as I could tell, did nothing but collect an ever-increasing annual trustee fee. The law has been relaxed so that the bank trust requirement only applies in "restricted zones," something to be checked out carefully. Another Mexican twist is that Mexico's laws have a bias in favor of the tenant, so buyers have to be careful about purchasing a house that is subject to a lease. The buyer may find it hard to terminate the lease, particularly if the tenant is a Mexican citizen. Then, thanks partly to Pancho Villa, there is a black hole for buyers known as *ejido* land. Following the Mexican Revolution the *ejido* system resulted in large amounts of land being dispersed communally to families in perpetuity. Such land should be avoided. But if you have a hankering to buy *ejido* land anyway, be prepared to meet the extended families of your soon-to- be new neighbors, rounding up their consents, going to membership meetings, and have the time, patience, and money to slog through a maze of Mexican laws that were decidedly not written for the benefit of land-buying tourists. There are other caveats, but here is one more – what to do about the gardener and maid that for years have been caring for the house you just bought. Unless you had the foresight to have the seller deal with them before closing, you can only hope that you will get along with your household staff, because if you don't, it can be costly to terminate them. Having said all of that, I had none of these problems with Lorenzo. And in all fairness to Mexico generally, we have bought and sold real estate there hassle-free.

The closing date for the Lorenzo deal was set a few weeks out to allow time for the customary title checks, surveys, and so forth. However, Lorenzo had a business plan that he failed to share with me. The plan was to buy a cow out of the closing proceeds and sell raw milk out of containers strapped to Lorenzo's burro. Apparently the business plan looked so compelling that Lorenzo started operations in partnership with his burro and the unpaid-for cow well in advance of our closing date. At that time I was back in Wisconsin tending to my law practice. I received a call from my broker that the cow had to be paid for before closing and would I please advance $500 so that Lorenzo and his partners (the burro and the cow) could stay in business. I, of course, agreed to that.

Well, the Lorenzo purchase closed timely and amicably. I built my garage and Lorenzo's milk route flourished. Lorenzo and I did have one post-closing glitch, however. One day before construction of the garage started, I had a rap on our front door. It was Lorenzo, smiling and jovial as ever. He wanted to know whether I intended to buy the large boulders that were embedded deep in the lot I had just purchased. I said: "Lorenzo, I think I already bought those boulders—they are, after all, part of the real estate." Then it dawned on me! This is Mexico. Maybe I don't own them. I told him to come back the next day to give me time to compose myself and consult with my builder. I was told by the builder that the boulders were useful (but not essential) to support the garage and that it would cost a fortune to remove them. I then knew in a flash how to unleash my vast legal talents on Lorenzo. I told him that construction starts tomorrow so remove your rocks quickly. He sure did not want to hear that. Then I said: "Okay Lorenzo, how much do you want for your rocks?" He said one hundred pesos (ten bucks, U.S.). The rock deal was concluded that instant. That was as close to a controversy as I ever had with that nice man.

The nine years that followed the purchase of the house were spent pouring pesos into it. It began cosmetically with the purchase of a huge portrait of a heavily armed Pancho Villa majestically mounted on his horse. While this original oil was patently shy of museum quality, it did serve as a lively centerpiece for the interior decorating to follow. It was not long thereafter, however, that the realization came that house problems were more mechanical and structural than they were aesthetic.

Enter now Armando and Rosendo. I met Armando for the first time just months after we bought the house. I was at the corner hardware shop struggling to explain to the shop owner my need for a few simple electrical products. The language barrier made this quite challenging. A nice man standing in the line behind me stepped forward to help. As fate would have it, Armando was a talented electrician and plumber, and he spoke some English. Better yet, at that time he was looking for work.

Over the years this chance encounter led to a lasting friendship, but it started that morning with Armando performing a legitimate home inspection. I was distressed, of course, to be told that the wiring was dangerous; that the toilet was not connected to the city sewer line; that the ceiling beams I thought were so charming were infested with termites, to name just a few of the most urgent items.

These revelations prompted me to reread the home inspection report I commissioned before buying the house. None of Armando's revelations was even so much as hinted at in the pre-closing report. To put it nicely, the home inspection business back then was not fully mature – at least not in this part of Mexico. The only items not found to be deficient were heating and air conditioning. That is because the house didn't have either. That was the bad news.

The good news was my loyal banker raised my credit limit and with that the rehab began. Armando soon enlisted the assistance of one Rosendo. Rosendo is perhaps one of the hardest working, most talented, and most underpaid tradesmen on the face of this earth. He is a mason whose tools consist of a trowel and a two-by-four. While I cannot say I know everything about his family, I do remember both of his sons were then in college studying music. He also had a daughter in business school. I knew then that if they are anything like their father, they will do well. And do well they did. On Sunday afternoon, October 21, 2012, Mary and I were seated in velvet cushioned seats at Guadalajara's historic *Teatro Delogollado* listening to a Brahms' composition performed by the Jalisco Philharmonic Orchestra. So was Rosendo. I spotted him beaming just one aisle forward and six seats to our right as his son, Manuel, in formal black attire, performed in the viola section. His other son, also an accomplished musician, teaches music. Rosendo reports that his daughter is doing well also. The construction business is slow where Rosendo lives so he now tends to a neighborhood shop selling snacks, fresh eggs, and some canned goods.

Armando and Rosendo rebuilt our house in spurts dictated largely by my cash flow. One spring day I flew down without Mary to oversee the projects then in progress. I know I arrived on the third of May even though I do not recall the year. May 3 is Día de la Santa Cruz, a national holiday for construction workers. When I walked through the door Armando and Rosendo were hard at work despite it being a holiday. I soon found out that this dedication came at a price. That evening there was to be a modest celebration honoring them on my patio. Being thus advised, I walked to the corner shop to buy a big jug of tequila, bottles of Squirt to serve as the mix, and most of the chips then on the display rack.

Having never before celebrated Dia de la Santa Cruz, I was not exactly certain what was expected of me. After the effects of a few shots of tequila and a full day of travel set in, I excused myself and went out for dinner alone. Upon returning an hour or so later, I found that the guest list had expanded to include a few helpers, friends, and family members, as well as a few of my neighbors whom I had yet to have the privilege of meeting. Back to the corner shop I went for more supplies with which to further honor Armando, Rosendo and Mexico's construction workers everywhere.

Sounds of Festivals

Big Bangs (Cohetes)

As remodeling progressed we turned more attention to our surroundings and less to the house. In the early years of home ownership we spent about six weeks in our Mexican house; by the last year this was stretched to nearly six months. Days merged into one another seamlessly as we became lured in to the sights, smells, and tastes around us. You will note that I omitted sounds. On that subject, dog owners and their dogs might consider getting as far from town as possible on local saint days.

Each village has its own annual fiesta in honor of its own patron saint. In our village of Ajijic this is a nine day fiesta occurring every November in honor of San Andrés (Saint Andrew). Saint Andrew was one of the disciples with Jesus at the Sea of Galilee where they encountered thousands of hungry followers on the hillside. Saint Andrew told Jesus about a boy who had five loaves of bread and two fish which he was willing to share. The story is told in four of the Gospels that a miracle then occurred and there was enough food for everyone.

The Bible also says that Saint Andrew not only found the boy who had the fish and the bread, Saint Andrew did a lot of other good things. That would explain why the folks of Ajijic celebrate the many festivities that occur in his honor; namely, processions, carnival rides, street decorations, amateur bands, and neighborhood eating and drinking on the street. If it were not for the blasting of cohetes for all nine days there would be no reason to miss the fun.

San Andrés Church and Village Square – Ajijic

© Enrique Velázquez / Lic.courtesy of Belva y Enrique Velázquez Studio, Ajijic • www.mymexicoart.com

Just a few miles to the east of San Andrés Church the citizens of Chapala honor their patron saint San Francisco (Francis of Assisi), the Italian friar who, in the thirteenth century, founded the Franciscan Order. He was also the friar who loved animals. Saint Francis is said to have tamed a wolf that had terrorized an entire village. Then Saint Francis made a deal with the town dogs that they would not bother the wolf so that everyone could live peaceably. The grateful townsfolk then lived in tranquility. But there is no tranquility in Chapala on October 4 of every year as the carnival in honor of San Francisco takes place. And there is no truce between Chapala's City Hall and the dogs of that city. At about 10:30 p.m. the fireworks begin – ready or not – and the town dogs start howling their heads off.

One has to wonder why rockets are such an essential part of fiesta days. The idea must be to "shock and awe" the saints, hoping the blasts will get the saints' attention and bestow blessings upon the villagers. But gunpowder wasn't discovered until about one thousand years after Saint Andrew died a martyr's death, and it was discovered by the Chinese. Gunpowder did not make its way into Europe until about the time Francis of Assisi was born and then it had to get there by camel or horse along the Silk Road. One might understand why gunpowder might be used to honor Confucius – but why Catholic saints? Mexicans never even heard of gunpowder until about five hundred years ago when the Conquistadors used it to shoot at the Aztecs.

But the sight of dogs cowering under the bursts of gunpowder pales into insignificance when compared with a few other Mexican pastimes.

The blood sport of cockfighting is not only legal in Mexico, it is a culturally acceptable activity in which two specially bred roosters (cocks) are held in a ring (cockpit) where their male aggressions make them battle it out it in a single round limited to 30 minutes. Many bouts end within a few sickening minutes. Almost all major Mexican cities have cockfighting arenas. Cockfights are often interspersed with singing and dancing performances. Some people feel there is a religious overlay to cockfighting because, since antiquity, the rooster has been a sacred animal in many cultures. But cockfighting in Mexico is anything but a godly event. Saint Francis would not have liked the sport. A lot of Mexicans don't like it either. The sport is regulated by the government, at least it is supposed to be.

And if Saint Francis were alive today, he would not cheer along with

40,000 others in Mexico City's Plaza México, the largest bullring in the world.[52] The four-hundred-year-old spectacle of bullfighting (fiesta brava) continues to be popular throughout much of Mexico despite world-wide sentiment against it. The bullfighting industry has at least 500 buildings or arenas in Mexico, more than 280 bullfighting breeding farms, and twelve bullfighting schools.[53] Fans argue that bullfighting is an art form like dance and music. Animal rights activists say it is atrocious and should be banned. One example animal activists cite is a religious festival in Tlacotalpan (Veracruz state) known as Embalse de Toros where seven or more bulls are forced to drink liquor and swim a river only to be tormented and then killed by hecklers hanging over the gunnels of small boats.[54] Like cockfighting, the bullfight may become a thing of the past. (There are efforts afoot in Mexico City to ban it). Until then, bullfighting and cockfighting take place in the same country where Francis of Assisi is venerated for his compassion for animals. So let's just say, as is repeatedly said, that Mexico is a country of contradictions.

Our dogs never understood contradictions, and we soon discovered they didn't understand the reasons for cohetes either. One year our elderly basset hound, Daffy, was struggling to stay alive. Putting Daffy to sleep was put on hold at every remote sign of her possibly getting better. We were unaware of the soon-to-begin San Andre festival. It started with a bang that shook our bed and startled our dogs. The bangs continued split seconds apart from rockets that seem to have been launched just outside our bedroom window. Our three dogs were terrified. Daffy was vomiting.

Because these fiestas are local and because different villages have different local saints, the festival's start and end dates vary from village to village. We therefore assumed that we could find peace in some other village. As the sun started breaking over the mountains Mary and I were assembling suit cases and dogs to evacuate until life in our village settled down. Not knowing where we were going meant that we did not know if we should pack for the mountains or for the beach. While we packed for both, we ended up five hours later at a quiet beach town on the Pacific called Cuyutlán in the state of Colima. We walked wood planks over the crusty black volcanic sand and scouted out the salty lagoon and mango trees said to provide sanctuary to hundreds of species of migratory birds. It being "off season" the town seemed abandoned despite signs of activity in the "catch of the day" food shanties that hugged the roaring surf. This is a place passed over for Puerto Vallarta and meccas like it – the perfect spot to wait out the havoc Saint Andrew was causing in Ajijic.

We found a modest hotel just a short distance from the sea and inquired whether our dogs would be welcome. No problem said the desk clerk – we were the hotel's only guests. Then the zinger: Were any festivals planned within the next week or so? Being told that he didn't know of any, I thought it best to do a little checking on my own. I had heard about the Charro-Taurino Feast, the state of Colima's most important festival. It is celebrated in honor of San Felipe de Jesús (Saint Philip) who protects the entire state of Colima against earthquakes and hurricanes. And, unlike San Francisco (from Italy) or San André (from Galilee), it happens that Felipe was from Mexico. I figured that such an important festival in honor of one of Mexico's own would be one whale of a hootenanny. But the desk clerk assured me that the San Felipe festival was held in the city of Villa de Alvarez, a considerable distance away and, in any event, it did not take place until February. Still, I was curious about the chap I was by then mistakenly calling "Felix."

It turns out that Felipe was born in 1572. He became restless in Mexico and took up life as a merchant in the Philippines (which, like Mexico, was then a Spanish colony). After a short stint there, Felipe decided to sail back to Mexico to be ordained as a Franciscan monk. However, his boat got caught in a storm that propelled the vessel upon the coast of Japan. The Japanese found ammunition on board and thought that the passengers and crew were orchestrating the early stages of an invasion against Japan. So Felipe slipped away to a Franciscan friary at present day Kyoto. But Felipe, along with other Franciscan friars, was arrested, imprisoned, paraded through Kyoto (with his ears cut off), taken to Nagasaki, bound upon a cross at the "Mount of the Martyrs," pierced with spears until he died.[55] It really is quite a tragic and compelling story and I am glad I looked into it. I can now see why Pope Pius IX canonized Felipe in 1862. And on a much less lofty plane, I was also satisfied that the townsfolk of Cuyutlán would not be honoring Felipe with cohetes – not while we would be there anyway.

The days in this seaside village went well with the exception of our otherwise passive border collie Sam who, while on an early morning walk with Mary, decided to attack a kitten sleeping under an unmanned vendor's cart. The next several hours were spent in the nearest town that had a veterinarian, some 30 minutes away. That's another story, but it will not be told here because we don't know how it ended. To this day I like to believe that the good vet had a little of Saint Francis in him and that the kitten found another cart to sleep under.

41

Daffy, the 15 year old basset hound, had a less encouraging future. She was soon to be put to sleep at the hands of another good vet, this one in Ajijic.

Our Dogs

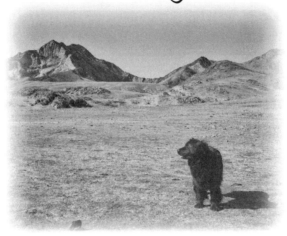

Cricket (Our Newfoundland)

Everyone connects Chihuahuas with Mexico. What most people probably don't know is that in ancient Aztec culture they were buried with their dead masters so that the master's sins would be transferred to the dog.[56] Chihuahuas, however, are relative newcomers to Mexico. The Xoloitzcuintliti ("Xolo"), sometimes referred to as the "Mexican Hairless Dog," were the first dog of the Americas.[57] Xolos are thought by some rural Mexicans to cure everything from rheumatism to toothaches. Our dog, Cricket (pictured above), would not be easily confused with either Chihauhuas or Xolos. – nor would our other dogs – about whom I will now tell you a bit more.

Sara, the "mean" one, was the first to go to Mexico. People in Mexico called her *Salchicha* because she looked like a sausage. We loved her anyway. She made three or four trips to Mexico before succumbing to old age – or perhaps it was a combination of dementia and exhaustion.

You already know something of Daffy, the bassett hound, and of Sam, the border collie. To round out our Mexico-era canine clan, you need to know at least something more about Cricket, the Newfoundland. As you might guess, Newfoundlands are not indigenous to Mexico. They are much too big and furry. Cricket nonetheless stoically tolerated the Mexican heat and the cramped conditions of traveling to and fro in our mid-sized car. Being a stray we had found on a lonely Wisconsin country road, she understood all too well that peaceful co-existence was the price of inclusion. Despite the lore that Newfoundlands find their true happiness saving fishermen stranded on ice bergs, Cricket's best Mexican moments were found helping Sam herd cows grazing on Lake Chapala's shores.

Oh yes, and then there is Frida. One morning while returning from the bakery at the end of our block, I encountered a very young puppy which, seconds before, had been swept out of an alley near our house by a very angry woman brandishing a broom. I figured it was probably best not to confront her. Accordingly, I left the situation unchallenged. However, while returning from dinner that evening my wife and I encountered a gathering of teenage girls near the same alley. One young lady was coddling the puppy. My wife made several inquiries. Does the puppy belong to any one of you? Do you know anything about her? Has she eaten today? Has she had water? Is anyone taking her home? All questions were answered in the negative except the next one. That question, posed by my wife, was whether we could bring her to our house. This street-side gathering voted in favor of my wife's proposition. The vote was unanimous only because I abstained. It being dark at the time we were not aware of the cloud of fleas over the puppy's head. Nor was this detected when she ended up above our pillows later that night. It was noticed big time as soon as the sun came up, however. It seemed an eternity before the neighborhood pet store and veterinary dispensary opened. When it did open, we were sold a magical powder that has to be illegal everywhere in the world. This stuff was amazing. One dose did the job. Frida remains flea-free to this day. I suspect the same can be said of all other dogs within a five mile radius of our house. Well, Frida, Cricket and Sam evolved into a closely-knit pack of three.

Year 2001

Frida grew to be a beautiful blend of collie, golden retriever, and spaniel and is fully Americanized.

The Indiginous People

*O*nce we felt settled in our remodeled house and had located a good place to board our dogs, we began to explore Mexico in earnest. We decided to start with the natives because they were there first.

Our younger son, while visiting Mexico with us during his college years, had this to say about ruins: "They don't get that name for nothing." He was referring to archaeological sites of Mexico. We have dragged him and his siblings through many of them. But he enjoyed being photographed with ancient pyramids in the background, and he was impressed by the huge stone palaces, temples, and ball courts found in the jungles, cloud forests, and plains of Mexico. Even he realized there was more to this history-rich country than pristine beaches and Corona beer.

There are thousands of known archaeological sites in Mexico. Only about forty-five have been scientifically excavated.[58] Many of those that have been excavated are open to the public. These are the remains of the fabled civilizations of ancient Mexico. While archaeologists have provided vast amounts of information about the sites, there remains a great deal more for their trowels to unearth. That is why, in and among the ruins, archaeological crews are on hands and knees in the blazing sun sifting through teaspoon size clumps of sand and dirt in hopes, against staggering odds, that they will brush clean some object – maybe a jade bead or a shard from a broken vase – that will put them a tiny bit closer to solving the mysteries of Mesoamerica's past. (Roughly speaking, "Mesoamerica" [Middle America] is the geological and cultural area from central Mexico through Central America).

The reason the natives of the American continent are called "Indians" is that Christopher Columbus thought he had landed in India when, in fact, he was on the shores of the Bahamas. Not being one to second-guess himself, he insisted on calling the islanders "Indians." The label stuck and spread throughout the New World, including into what is now Mexico. Columbus could have blamed others for his blunder. People in Europe then referred to much of eastern Asia as "India," and, *lo and behold,* the ancestors of the people he called "Indians" actually came from Asia. It's just that Columbus didn't know that – and, at the time, nobody else did either.

The ancient forefathers of Mexico's purebred Indians, like the natives of the American continent generally, crossed from Asia over the frozen Bering Straits and, over many thousands of years, populated both continents deep into South America. They are believed to have come in waves. The first wave of Asians could date back as early as 40,000 BCE.[59] By 9000 BCE the ice that had covered the Bering Straits melted and migration over the Straits stopped.[60]

The migrants were hunters and gatherers. The nomadic life they led was hard and dangerous. However, the technology of hunting took a huge turn for the better about 10,000 BCE with the invention of the stone point.[61] Big game hunters then could spear hairy mammoths and giant armadillos, particularly if the ancient beasts got bogged down in the muck of lakebeds. Even then it was a dangerous way to get meat. Take the case of the "Tepexpan Man" whose skeleton was discovered in the late 1940's near present day Mexico City. The "man" appears to have met a violent death when he was charged by a raging mastodon.[62] "Man" is in quotation marks because he is now believed to have been a woman.

The huge prehistoric creatures of the wild started to disappear about 7500 BCE as vegetation that fed them started to dry up.[63] The hunters then turned to smaller game.

Hunting and gathering continued, but as early as 5000 BCE the gatherers experimented with farming.[64] With the advent of farming, life on the move started to give way to life on the farm. By about 2000 BCE corn (maize) became the main source of human subsistence.[65] Corn proved to be an ideal staple for conditions in Mesoamerica. Unlike rice and wheat, corn was easy to grow. Farmers cultivated the soil with crude bone and steel tools and later learned to fertilize by "slashing and burning."

The impact of farming was profound. Farming meant that not everybody had to work full-time just to feed themselves. At least some people were able to do other things – to learn the mysteries of the heavens – to figure out the seasons – to build buildings – to make pots that were beautiful as well as useful – to make jade earrings and necklaces – to develop a written language – to sculpt stone figures – to trade their crafts and farm products with neighboring villages – to make war – and, to worship their gods. These were just some of the key features of the so-called "Formative Period" that started about 2000 BCE and ended about 300 CE. It was during the "Formative Period" that the foundation for the great civilizations of Mesoamerica was laid and political, social and economic structures evolved.

The "Formative Period" ushered in the period known as the "Classic Period" (300 CE-900 CE). It was during the Classic Period that the accomplishments of the Formative Period were brought together, advanced to new heights, and reached their intellectual and artistic peak (sometimes called the "Golden Age"). The civilizations of the "Golden Age" are best known for their magnificent palaces, pyramids, and temples; the corbeled arch; a calendar more accurate than any in Europe; the mathematical concept of zero.

Many parts of the world were then anything but "Golden." There were pockets of darkness all over this earth: Atilla the Hun had swept through western Europe; Rome had gone from decline to collapse; in England, the Pope had tried to make Christians out of illiterate Anglo–Saxons. Yet beacons of light shone brightly from the "Golden" civilizations of Mesoamerica – as they did from China's Tang Dynasty (618 CE-906 CE), Justinian's Byzantine empire (482 CE-565 CE), and elsewhere. But the lights of Mesoamerica were soon to burn out, and the proof of what made these civilizations "Golden" was buried, not to be discovered until centuries later.

What the great civilizations of Mesoamerica left behind would astonish a Spanish Captain by the name of Antonio del Río. In 1787 he was sent on an expedition by King Charles III to report on the incredible achievements rumored to have occurred in New Spain centuries before New Spain became a Spanish colony. Antonio was so overwhelmed by what he found he concluded that ancient Romans, Egyptians, or perhaps the Greeks, must have gotten to Mexico before Spain got there. The King must not have wanted to hear that because Antonio's findings were stashed away in an archive in Madrid and were not published until over thirty years later. That aside, Antonio's report about the wonders of Mexico's ancient civilizations proved to be right—what proved to be wrong was thinking the Romans, Egyptians or Greeks had anything to do with creating them, but on this, not everyone agrees.

A Mayan Pyramid

So we ask: What caused these remarkable communities to be scattered throughout Mexico's river valleys, jungles, and plateaus? In those days there was no concept of a nation. Each community covered an area only as big as its ruler could control. We now call them "city-states." With few exceptions, each city-state was populated by people whose cultural origins and language were similar; for example, each of the many Mayan city-states was populated by Mayan speaking people who traced their origins to a common background. Stated yet another way, there were many city-states and each one had a dominant ethnic and linguistic identity.

A scholar devoting a lifetime to studying just one of the ancient civilizations of Mexico would find it abhorrent to tell the stories of the major cultures on a single page map. I shall bulldoze ahead anyway – such a map is on the following page:

Ancient Civilizations of Mexico

❶ Olmecs: First major civilization of Mesoamerica – 1500 BCE - 400 BCE. The "Mother Culture." Noted for artwork (colossal 8 foot-40 ton stone heads, jade masks, animal figurines); pioneered writing, calendar, astronomy; engaged in human sacrifice, played ball games and were long distance traders.

❷ Mayans: 400 BCE - 900 CE. "City Builders." Discussed in this Chapter 7.

❸ Zapotecs: 500 BCE created capital city of Monte Alban on a leveled off mountain top in Oaxaca valley. By 450 CE controlled much of southern Mexico. Decline began about 700 CE. By 1521 population plummeted and scattered, and then rebounded to one of today's largest indigenous groups in Mexico.

❹ Mixtecs: The "Cloud (Mountain) People." Peaked about 900 CE - 1200 CE . Replaced Zapotecs as the region's power. Noted for codices (deerskin books).

❺ Teotihuacán: A major city begun about 100 BCE by an amalgam of cultures (or, possibly Toltecs). It thrived until about 700 CE – became one of the largest cities in the world (bigger than Rome). Bustling economy. Grand avenues and pyramids. Destroyed by invasion or burning.

❻ Toltecs: About 968 CE the Toltecs moved their capital from Teotihuacán to Tula. Flourished until 12th century.

❼ Aztecs: 1300 CE – 1521 CE. Discussed at Chapter 8.

I trust that by now any true scholars reading this book gave up some pages back. To the few who may be too stunned to have stopped, I give them this fair warning: I am about to portray the shining years of one ancient Mayan city-state – well, at least, a little something about one of them. To perform this daunting task, I have chosen Palenque, situated in the mountainous rain forests of the Mexican state of Chiapas.

For those who have vacationed on Mexico's Caribbean coast, Palenque is about a one day drive from either Cancún or Riveria Maya. For those who may not be familiar with these vacation meccas, Chiapas borders Guatemala.

Be aware, however, that Palenque is in thick jungle so you will want to get better directions before going there. What you will be looking for is a ledge in the foothills of the misty Tumbalá mountains from which one can see swampy plains that reach all the way to the Gulf Coast, and where one can hear the howling monkeys of the jungle. But it is the awesome remains of the ancient city of Palenque – not the plains and not the monkeys – that trump everything in sight.

Palenque was one of about forty Mayan communities spread across modern day Mexico, Guatemala, and northern Belize. At the peak of the Mayan civilization there were about two million Mayan people. The Mayan people first appeared in the lush jungles of southern Mexico about 400 BCE.

Palenque is believed to have been started about 100 BCE and soon flourished. This is more than a story about Palenque, however – it is also a story about its most famous king, Pakal the Great. He became king of Palenque in 603 CE. It probably will not surprise you to learn that he has since passed away, but it may surprise you to learn that he is still there – buried in the "Temple of Inscriptions."

In 1840 a travel writer by the name John Lloyd Stephens and an artist/architect named Frederick Catherwood, accompanied by native guides, ventured into the steaming jungle on mules to uncover the secrets of "The Lost City of Palenque." Actually, Palenque was never really *lost.* The locals knew about it all along. So did some foreigners. It was the drenching rains, swarms of mosquitoes, and poisonous snakes that kept others from digging into its secrets. But that didn't faze Stephens and Catherwood. They slogged and fought through it all and went on to find the "Lost City," map it, and document Catherwood's renderings. Stephens wrote a book called *Incidents of Travel in Central America, Chiapas and Yucatán* that inspired the likes of Edgar Allan Poe and captured the attention of the world.

While Stephens and Catherwood put Palenque on the map, they missed a find that over a century later would make a director of research for Mexico's Instituto National de Arqueología y Historia world-famous. His name was Alberto Ruz Lhuiller.

Ruz had been exploring the nooks and crannies of the "Temple of Inscriptions" for years when, in 1952, he made the discovery of a lifetime. He followed a dark and dusty stairwell down some eighty feet to a vaulted room at the end of the stairs. There he realized that the walls in the room extended below the stone floor. (To 'who dun it' buffs, it was a fake floor!) Under the fake floor was a chamber that looked to Ruz to be an abandoned chapel. Ruz later wrote, "...out of the dim shadows [emerged] a sight from another world." [The chamber was] "...filled with a great carved stone slab, in perfect condition..." Ruz was beholding a sight not seen by anyone for over a thousand of years – it was a magnificent tomb that Ruz knew held the remains of a very great ruler of Palenque.

The next mystery was to figure out who was in the tomb Ruz discovered. It was soon determined that the tomb was the tomb of K'inich Janaab' Pakal, the best known of Palenque's kings. Some are skeptical because the remains appear to be of a younger man, but most scholars think – like the old gag about Grant's tomb – Pakal is in Pakal's tomb. Ruz must have thought so because he later chose to be buried in the shade of some trees not far from Pakal the Great.

Pakal's bones were draped in a suit of precious jade connected by gold wire. His face was covered with a mask carved from jade. His tomb contained offerings worth a fortune. One might ask what made Pakal *great* other than his wealth? Well, for starters, he must have *thought* he was *great*. He was the one who ordered the pretentious 'Temple of Inscriptions' to be built to house his elaborate tomb. Chances are, too, that he had something to do with designing the fake floor. He also must have thought that Palenque would be in trouble without the benefit of his sage counsel – so he had a tube built into the temple so he could talk to his priests from his grave.

Throughout history, kings, potentates, dictators, and presidents have burnished their images by building great buildings and edifices. Pakal was no exception. Unlike the usual Mayan succession to the Crown, Pakal was the son of a reigning Queen and it was she who passed the Crown to her son Pakal as soon as he reached "maturity" at age twelve. But it was not his young age that people cared about; they questioned whether a queen could pass the crown at all. Most Mayan crowns passed from a king to the king's oldest son. But Pakal was crowned anyway. He managed to hold the kingship until he died at age eighty, even though he continually had to fend off challenges to his right to reign. He held off his distractors by building grand buildings, temples, and edifices – in Washington parlance, "pork." These grand monuments are what helped to make Pakal *great.* But what also made Pakal *great* was the widespread belief that he was a descendant of the Mayan gods.

Here I must stray from archaeologically-based facts to something more fanciful – the legend of the "Hero Twins." [66] The story is a magical account of how twin brothers, who were excellent athletes, were lured into the underworld by the Lords of the Underworld and then were able to persuade a Lord to cut himself into pieces. (The "trick" was to put the pieces back together – if the magic worked – which it did not.) The Lords of the Heaven were pleased that the Lords of the Underworld had been duped and rewarded the Twins by making one of them the Sun and the other the Moon.The part of the story the Mayan kings liked best was that descendants of the Hero Twins were to rule the Mayans thereafter. As long as people believed that, the easier it was to pass the dynasty down to the next generation – and to stay in power for life. The legend of the Hero Twins helped – the magnificent buildings, statuary, and royal "pomp and circumstance" provided the rest.

Pakal was an absolute ruler. His palace was a complex of stone buildings with throne rooms, courtyards, an observation tower, baths, and saunas. A river was diverted to flow beneath the palace to provide the palace with water. The palace walls were painted brightly, mostly in red but also in blue, yellow, and white. The halls, rooms, and courtyards were graced with bas-relief carvings and elaborate stone sculptures. Life in the royal court was one of luxury and privilege. Nobles adorned themselves with jewelry and tunics made from the fur of jaguars. The king sat on an elegant throne while vassals knelt before him. Scribes kept count of the tribute that poured in – feathers, cocoa beans, and bundles of fine clothes. The king was entertained by dwarfs and jesters.

There can only be one king at a time. It took others to make up a kingdom. Pakal looked to his priests for advice. They were the keepers of knowledge and knew when to plant, when to go to war, which were the lucky days, and which were the unlucky days. Pakal also needed craftsmen to make the beautiful fabrics, jade earrings, necklaces, and fine pottery that surrounded him. Pakal also needed warriors to protect what he had, to add to it, and to capture enemies to be used as slaves. Pakal needed laborers to build his great buildings. And, of course, he and his people had to eat, so his great city was surrounded with farms.

Farmers and commoners lived on the periphery of Palenque, usually in one room huts built with poles and covered with mud. A typical family had five to seven members. Their meals were corn, beans, squash, avocados, tomatoes—sometimes turkey, monkey, rabbit, deer, pigs. Women weaved and cooked. They ground corn and made tortillas. In the evening the heads of the households would chant and pray to their ancestors, who often were buried below the floor of their hut. They tied boards to the foreheads of newly born babies to form flat foreheads. To be cross-eyed was a thing of beauty, so mothers dangled objects before the noses of their babies.

Social life consisted of attending royal marriages or ceremonies involving the calendar or celestial events. There were ball games played in courts that had a stone ring. Each team's objective was to get the heavy solid rubber ball through the ring. They took their games quite seriously; in fact some members of the losing team lost more than the game – they lost their lives. Some say it was the winning team that was put to death; nobody seems to know for sure.

Pakal and his people (rich friends only) had a fondness for a chocolate mushy concoction which to them was the "Drink of the Gods." Poor people couldn't afford it – but they had *ixtac octli* (their 'white lighting') made from the juicy sap of the maguey cactus plant.

Historians suggest that drinking alcohol was limited to ritual ceremonies and was strictly regulated. I am not so sure. In 1969 a 165 foot long mural was unearthed in nearby Cholula at the site of a very big ancient pyramid. The mural, which archaeologists call "The Drunkards," portrays partying with what may have been pulque, an alcoholic beverage popular in Mexico today.[67] Not everyone agrees that it was pulque, however; it may have been a "hallucinogenic potion derived from mushrooms or peyote." [68] And they may not have been partying at all; it could have been a ritual ceremony.

Appearances have been important throughout history. Mayans were no exception. Men (i.e., males who had reached the age of passage, usually age 12) wore a *maxtlatl*, a cloth wrapped around the lower torso and passed between the legs – the ends of the cloth were then tied around the waist. The *timatli* was a cape worn over the shoulders. These could be quite elaborate, with brilliant embroidered designs of scorpions and jaguars, and they could be laced with conch shells. They were used to signal one's station and rank. Rich men had many of them. In fact, they could be traded as currency. Thirty could buy you a slave. Forty would buy you a slave that could sing and dance.

Women wore brightly colored skirts down to the ankles and a blouse called a *huipil*, often woven in designs that displayed where they were from or their marital status. Sandals were worn by both sexes. Sandals were needed to enter the temple. The Mayan ensemble was completed with feathered head dresses that defy description – so I will not attempt one. This is what they looked like:

Palenque's glory days were numbered. There was no new construction in Palenque after 800 CE. Many inhabitants started drifting elsewhere and those who stayed mostly farmed. No one knows why Palenque disintegrated – maybe ecological self-destruction, maybe it had to do with the loss of trade routes. In time, cedar, mahogany and sapodilla saplings took root in Palenque's abandoned plazas and mountain weeds crept over its great palaces, temples and pyramids. Then the ravages of time, vandalism, and thievery took their tolls.

Sooner or later the other ancient civilizations of Mesoamerica suffered Palenque's fate. By the 14th century it was up to the Aztecs to save the indigenous culture. But the Aztecs fell to the Conquistadors in 1521, and so ended an era in Mexico that started thousands of years earlier. Yet today one out of every ten Mexicans is of pure indigenous stock – and nearly all Mexicans trace part of their ancestry to the ancient civilizations of Mexico.

Before leaving the subject of the ancient civilizations, passing mention has to be made as to why, as Antonio del Río observed, the pyramids in Mexico look so much like those in Egypt. The "look alike" question is hotly debated. So, too, is the debate between the biblical version of creation and Darwinian evolution. While the debate about evolution deeply divides many people, almost all people agree that mankind has been around for thousands and thousands of years. Conventional wisdom holds that the "great" civilizations of the world had their start sometime around 3000 BCE in the middle-eastern part of the world, and that the great civilizations of Mexico and other parts of Mesoamerica started later. The question, then, is this: Did these civilizations on opposite sides of two immense oceans spring up free from the influence of each other? Some folks don't go along with the Bering Straits explanation. They contend that early people came to the American continent by boat from the South Pacific; others will argue they came from southwestern Europe (Iberian Peninsula).[69]

Still others cling to the notion that a technologically advanced and unknown society once existed that traveled to far distant places, knew a lot about those places, and then disappeared from the face of the earth. Speculating about a "lost civilization" is nothing new. In 370 BCE Plato wrote about a great military power that came from a huge island, but he didn't say just where it was, and neither he nor others took the legend seriously. But in recent times, theories abound of a lost ancient civilization that some people take very seriously. One example: the book, *Fingerprints of the Gods,* refers to a map prepared in Constantinople in 1513 that depicts, among other things, the northern coast of Antarctica in an ice-free condition. It has been theorized (for reasons beyond the scope of this chapter) that the 1513 map drew on *earlier* maps that were made *before* 4000 BCE.[70] If that is true, explorers from a lost civilization may have navigated the world and charted it long before there were pyramids in either Egypt or Mexico. And if that is true, perhaps this lost civilization was the primogenitor of the Mayans and the other great civilizations of antiquity, thus accounting for haunting similarities in art, architecture, theology, and astronomy that once existed between the ancient civilizations. Many scholars scoff at such arguments. They reject the notion that a lost civilization remains hidden somewhere on the floor of some ocean.

Maybe the reason many remain puzzled is that the speculation has been too close to the planet Earth. Some prefer to look to outer space. They see something bizarre in the elaborate inscriptions on the lid of Pakal's tomb. What they see is a depiction of a man seated at the controls of a capsule hurtling through space. That man is "The Astronaut of the Temple of Palenque." Sound far-fetched? Maybe so –but there are plenty of UFO theorists who would argue the point.[71] Experts know that in Mayan legend there was a god from the "other side" by the name of Votan. The "other side" could, of course, mean heaven or hell, as the Mayans believed in both. Or, it could mean a strange and distant land. But could the "other side" mean outer space? Why is it that the remains in Pakal's tomb appear to have non-Mayan features? Why is the pyramid in Palenque the only one found in the new world with an Egyptian-like tomb? How was it possible for the Mayans to know so very much about mathematics, the stars, and engineering? Could aliens from outer space have visited Palenque and other ancient cultures of our world? And why did Mayan culture collapse? Could the people of Palenque have been abducted by extra-terrestrial beings?

Do not expect answers to these questions – not in this book anyway.

The End of Indian Dominion

Lic:/ istockphoto

Moctezuma II

The glory days of Palenque had been long over and their people had scattered when, in the fourteenth century, a nomadic tribe, *Mexica* (pronounced 'may-SHEE-ka'), and better known as Aztec, started to rise to power. By the time the Spanish arrived in 1519 the Aztecs were by far the most dominant of the Indian people. Others of the great civilizations had dispersed or vanished.

Every Mexican schoolchild is taught the story of Cortés and Moctezuma and how, in 1521, a small band of Conquistadors conquered the mighty Aztec empire. Volumes have been written on both sides of the Atlantic of how that event changed history.

But should you want to conjure up the spectacle of these times, there is no better place than the rooftop restaurant of the Majestic Hotel in Mexico City's historic section. Ask for a table near a window. It's not the fanciest hotel in Mexico, but the view is nothing short of majestic. From your table you will look out over the *Plaza de la Constitución,* the largest public square in the western hemisphere. The huge Mexican flag that towers over the plaza bears the emblem of an eagle perched on a cactus. A serpent is in the eagle's beak. Aztec legend has it that the gods instructed the Aztecs to found their city where such an eagle appeared. The eagle must have perched where the flag now flies because that is where, in 1335, the Aztecs built their magnificent capitol city of Tenochtitlan.

Tenochtitlan was Mexico's version of Venice. It was on an island in Lake Texcoco. The lake has since gone dry, but, at the time Moctezuma ruled the Aztecs, the lake served as a moat to protect the city. The island was connected to the mainland by causeways. Canoes ferried people and cargo over a network of canals within the city and over the lake to nearby villages. It was a city of great wealth with shining, whitewashed palaces, grand buildings, a zoo, ball courts, and gardens. Its pyramids were brightly painted. Nobles lived in two story homes with as many as 50 rooms.[72] Its main temple, *Templo Mayor,* had two towers, one dedicated to *Tlaloc,* the god of rain, and the other to *Huitzilopochtli,* the god of war. Each had a separate staircase leading to a shrine at the top. Aqueducts supplied fresh water to the city. Sewage was collected on barges and transported to the fields as fertilizers. The island was surrounded by man-made floating gardens. Tenochtitlan was as advanced as any city then in Europe. It was one of the largest urban centers in the world. It covered more than four square miles and had an estimated population of 200,000, putting it in a league with the likes of Paris, Venice, Milan and Naples.[73] One of the Conquistadors, Bernal Díaz del Castillo, described Tenochtitlan as the Garden of the World. [74] No wonder he was in awe. Seville, the Spanish city from which the Conquest was launched, then had a population of just 40,000.[75]

February 18, 1519, was likely to have been just another day for

Moctezuma as he sat down for dinner in his opulent palace while three thousand servants presented him with a choice of one hundred dishes from which to select. At least that is what Moctezuma's daily menu was reputed to have been.[76] It was good that he had his mind on eating because, on that day, Hernán Cortés, together with 550 of his men, 300 Indians, 16 horses, 10 brass guns, and a cannon set sail on eleven tall ships from the island of Cuba on a mission that would change Moctezuma's life and alter the history of the world. It would be just a matter of time before the "bearded white men with crosses" [77] would make their way from the coast to pay Moctezuma a visit.

Imagine the tales Moctezuma's scouts told their King about the Conquistadors' tall boats, guns, and horses. Moctezuma was in a quandary. He most certainly could have snuffed out the uninvited guests the moment they landed. But he did not. Moctezuma had been hearing from his prophets of the impending doom of his great Aztec empire. Perhaps this was the beginning of an apocalypse. Then there was the legend of the Aztec God Quetzalcóatl who had sailed away long ago and promised to return and reclaim his land. Had Quetzalcóatl himself returned? Were these strangers his descendants? Or were the intruders just ordinary mortals? Hoping they might be just mortals, he tried to buy them off with gifts, but that failed. The next step was to meet with Cortés.

Cortés had concerns of his own. He was greatly outnumbered. He had burned his boats to prevent the Conquistadors from deserting. What choices did Cortés have?

The two leaders sounded each other out and eventually a meeting was arranged between them. Imagine the moment when they met: Cortés in shining armor crossing Tenochitlan's drawbridge on his horse; Moctezuma waiting in elegant native dress, surrounded by his royal entourage; each figure outwardly imposing and proud – each inwardly afraid. They exchanged gifts, but the thousands looking on knew that the offerings they bestowed on each other were hollow gestures. War was in the making.

The story, of course, ends with the fall of Tenochtitlan. It fell on August 13, 1521, after prodding and sabre rattling erupted into a real war. Moctezuma was by then dead (having been killed by a rock perhaps thrown at him by one of his own people – or perhaps hurled by a Conquistador – or perhaps he was slain at the direction of Cortés). The palaces, temples, and plazas of once splendid Tenochtitlan lay in ruins. The same Conquistador who earlier described the city as a "garden" lamented that, of all the wonders he beheld, nothing remains; all is "overthrown and lost." [78]

But, the Aztecs didn't need to be told that their magnificent city lay in shambles and that it would never return. And they knew all too well that Tenochtitlan belonged to the victors. What the Aztecs didn't know was how dreadful their lives would be under colonial rule.

Tenochtitlan Memorial

The Colony

Mexico's Flag Towering Over Plaza de la Constitución

$\mathcal{S}$hould you be spending the night at the Majestic Hotel, forget about a wake-up call, particularly if your room overlooks the *Plaza de la Constitución.* The Mexican Army will see to it that you do not sleep through breakfast. At precisely six o'clock in the morning sixteen soldiers (by my count) parade single file onto the plaza with an enormous rolled-up flag hoisted upon their right shoulders. An army band brings up the rear with drums rolling and trumpets blaring.

This is the daily raising of the flag – at least, that is how the Mexican flag is raised in the *Plaza de la Constitución.* The jumbo green, white and orange national banner is then unfolded in rigid military pageantry and run up an immense steel pole that towers over the plaza. And, the band plays on. No one should want to sleep though this dignified and impressive ceremony, even if it were possible – which it is not. (The bonus for getting up so early is having a cocktail on the balcony exactly twelve hours later to watch the flag go down.)

Instead of going back to bed it is fun to watch the city awake. Looking straight out from your balcony is the National Palace.

The Palace consumes the east side of the plaza and it is the seat of the executive branch of government, including the office of Mexico's President. It stands on the site where Moctezuma once reigned over the Aztec Empire.

National Palace

Looking left from your balcony is the *Metropolitan Cathedral of the Assumption of Mary of Mexico,* better known as "The National Cathedral," the oldest and biggest cathedral in the Americas. Its ornate twin bell towers loom over the plaza. The cathedral stands on the sacred site of Tenochtitlan's main temple, *Templo Mayor.*

Kevin Willert

National Cathedral

It is a short walk from the Majestic's lobby to where Aztec nobles once had their large and fine homes. In their place now stand graceful old buildings that once were the stately mansions of well-to-do Spanish colonists. One well known example is *The House of Tiles,* now a popular restaurant and retail shop.

This is the Plaza as it is today. There is little left of the Aztec world that can be seen from your hotel balcony (even though archaeologists are constantly doing "digs" in the area). Preservationists the Conquistadors were not. They set out to transform the Indian world into a world that would look just like Spain. Their plan was to get rid of everything "Indian." That meant trashing the Aztecs' temples and pyramids; bringing in Europe's finest architects and urban planners; erecting Catholic churches and noblemen's mansions on top of the rubble.

Tenochtitlan got more than just a face lifting, however. It soon was to get a new name – Mexico – derived from *Mexica.* It was from this renamed Aztec city that Spain was to rule Mexico, Central America (except Panama), the Spanish West Indies, and the southwestern United States – together, "New Spain."

The King appointed Cortés as Governor of New Spain. But the Crown soon became suspicious of Cortés and surrounded him with persons the King knew he could trust. Cortés must have known that he was headed for early retirement when he was offered the title of *Marqués del Valle de*

Oaxaca and was awarded a hefty golden parachute consisting of, among other things, a grant of rights to tribute from 23,000 Indians. Such a grant was known as an *encomienda*.

The King replaced Cortés with a *Viceroy* (Vice-King) who, unlike Cortés, was of royal blood. The Viceroy was to serve as the King's personal representative. Keeping things in the royal family seemed like a safe bet.

It was not easy managing a colony from the other side of the Atlantic. Messages went back and forth on slow-sailing boats that were at the peril of storms and pirates. When reports from New Spain finally did arrive, the response from the Crown was often bogged down in ceremony and indecision.

King Charles V had known for some time that he needed help ruling Spain's colonies. In 1524 he created the *Council of the Indies* – an oversight and advisory committee of high-ranking Spaniards charged with managing colonial affairs. In 1527 the King established an *audiencia* in Mexico, it being a panel of judges that also had legislative and executive powers.

As time went on and frontiers expanded, the King split the colony into territorial units known as *corregimientos.* The purpose was to create an administrative bureaucracy that would be responsive to the King. But as the government grew, it became unwieldy and corrupt. So, the King had undercover people keep eyes on the systems the King had put in place. They were royal inspectors (*visitadores*).

The Spanish Crown outlawed slavery. But there was a loophole. An *encomienda* was a grant by the Spanish Crown to a "deserving" colonist (often a Conquistador) of certain property rights over a group of as many Indians as the grant specified. The grantee (*encomiendero*) became entitled to tribute from those Indians – in labor, gold, and other goods. That way the colonist did not actually own the Indian and therefore the laborer was not a slave. Sound unfair? Not if you believe the *encomiendero* was obliged to protect his Indian wards, teach them Spanish, and instruct them in the Catholic faith.

But the King suspected foul play. He was not terribly surprised when his *visitadores* reported corruption and incompetence, but he was furious when he was told that the *encomiendero* system had reduced the natives to virtual slaves. The King had looked upon the system originally as pension for the Conquistadors (and other worthy subjects of the Crown) and as a way to make Christians out of natives. But the system had turned evil. While it eventually was abandoned, it never fully went away. It was the forerunner of *haciendas* that fueled the Mexican Revolution of 1910.

The Conquistadors were mostly rough-and-tumble types who, when they signed on with Cortés, had little to lose by taking a long shot at wealth and fortune. They were not searching for a patch of farmland where they could practice their faith free of religious tyranny.

Later waves of newcomers from Spain were more genteel. But any way one looked at it, the Spanish were drastically outnumbered. Thus, it behooved the Spanish to install a social order that would compensate for their minority status. They were not content, however, to merely "level the playing field." People of pure Spanish blood wanted a race-based system skewed to favor them. The King obliged.

At the top of the system were the *Peninsulares*. They were white folks who were born in Spain and who relocated to New Spain. Below them were white Spaniards born in Mexico (*Criollos*). After the "whites," the system worked down to people of mixed color. A *Mestizo* was of mixed Spanish-Indian blood; a *Mulatto* was a Spanish-Negro mix. Native Indians were at the bottom – except that slaves imported from Africa were at the very bottom. The system got hopelessly confusing. And, it meant more than just who one's friends would be or what parties one could attend. Nonwhites could not hold certain government jobs, become clerics, carry arms, nor serve in the military.[79] They were not even supposed to wear "fine clothes."

The system was intended to do more than enshrine the notion of Spanish superiority. It created a labor pool of "lesser" people to cater to whites and to generate wealth for the mother country. But there was a glitch – there was a shortage of Spanish women. As a consequence, many male Spaniards had to decide either to marry an Indian woman or "live in sin" against the dictate of the Church. Here the Church and the King did not see eye-to-eye. The Church favored intermarriage as it was an easy way to convert Indians to Christianity. The King favored maintaining the purity of the Spanish race and encouraged Spanish whites only to marry each other.

The system proved to be a can of worms. Before a baby could be baptized the priest had to decide the caste to which the child would be assigned. The determination was no minor matter – at least not for the baby. The infant's lifetime status hung in the balance of the priest's verdict at the baptismal font. How tempting it must have been for the anxious parents to slip a silver coin or two into the priest's robe! Corruption of the clergy was not the only consequence of the caste system. Back then there were few ways a woman could improve her situation other than to marry into a class higher than her own. Thus, for example, a beautiful young *Criollo* maiden (born in the colony) would have been well counseled to keep a lookout for a handsome (and preferably, rich), young *Peninsular* groom (born in Spain). Their marriage would vastly improve the bride's station in life even though her *Criollo* status remained. So, what was wrong about marrying *up*? The problem was that *Criollo* women found it easier to marry up than did their male counterparts, thus creating a shortage of unmarried Criollo women. The result: many *Criollo* men were forced to marry *down*. This in turn meant that their children would be demoted to a status that could make them ineligible by law from seeking the job of their choice, and so forth.

There were issues at the upper end too. Being born in New Spain *(Criollos)* carried a stigma because the "atmosphere of New Spain produced beings who were physically, mentally, and morally inferior"[80] to persons born in Europe *(Peninsulares)*. Being born surrounded by the refinements of Europe somehow made one a better person than being born in a "backward" colony. That kind of nonsense just made matters worse.

Many *Peninsulares* and *Crillos* acquired great wealth. Some doled out their money to the Crown in exchange for titles like *Conde* or *Marquis*. Some gave out of a genuine sense of philanthropy, like Don José de la Borda. He was from Taxco, the silver capital of Mexico. After Borda struck a rich silver vein (actually, he struck many), he proclaimed *"God gives to Borda and Borda gives to God."* Borda kept his end of the bargain: after building roads and bridges and beautifying his city by giving free red roof tiles to his neighbors, Borda bankrolled Taxco's church of Santa Prisca, one of the most beautiful Baroque style churches in all of Mexico.[81]

Borda's Gift to Taxco

Many of the wealthy had become quite cosmopolitan. Their social life was patterned after that of upper European society. For the gentlemen, "full dress" meant knee breeches, cutaway tailored coats over satin waistcoats, tricorn hats, powdered wigs, silk stockings, and leather shoes with silver buckles. For gentlewomen, the "conical shape" with hoop skirts was the "in thing." Women flaunted jewelry and fine apparel tailored from exquisite fabrics shipped from Asia and Europe. Women's hair was piled high and their hatbands were jeweled.

Among the elite, there was a demand for all fine European things, from ornate home furnishings to carriages. Women maneuvered through the crowds in elegant sedan chairs carried by slaves. The well-off traveled and studied in Europe, read poetry, and held discussions about politics and art.

Paintings were prized by Mexico's upper crust. Literature, poetry, music, sculpture and other of the arts thrived wherever the elite of New Spain lived. They knew how to entertain extravagantly with formal balls and dinners. They attended the latest plays and music recitals. Rich men played chess and gambled. They had plenty of leisure time for both. There were some eighty-five religious holidays to be celebrated, say nothing of local saint days and other festivities that had to be honored as well.

Everyone loves a parade and the colonists were no exception. Parades were often led by Indian chiefs clothed in full native regalia. Following them on horseback might be church and government officials; then would come clowns, jugglers, musicians and floats.

Today the most visible evidence of colonization is found in Mexico's architecture. It was to be expected that the colonists would replicate the buildings of Spain. In early colonial days architecture was a mix of Romanesque, Gothic, and Moorish. Later, the Spanish Renaissance impacted the look of buildings with intricate plasterwork fashioned after the work of silversmiths, called "plateresque." Then architecture moved to "ultra baroque," a style of extraordinarily busy ornamentation.

Colonial life had its dark side, of course. Only the "few" lived and played in the manner imagined from your hotel balcony. Crime plagued the streets and roadways. Criminals were hanged to death and their bodies were strung along the roadside. Others were drawn and quartered and the human parts put on display. For lesser offenses, the punishment was mutilation of a limb or crushing a foot in a "boot." Beggars were everywhere. Thousands of lepers roamed the capitol city in tattered clothes. Epidemics were common, particularly smallpox. Life expectancies were short. People aged quickly and often smelled bad. Surgeons typically were barbers.

On the stairwell walls of the National Palace the mural by Diego Rivera depicts Mexico's unending history of turmoil and suffering, including the rape, torture, and ugliness of the Conquest, the enslavement of the Indians, the battle for independence from Spain, foreign invasions, and the Revolution of 1910 and its aftermath. The mural is called "The Epic of the Mexican People." That epic began right where the doorman at the Majestic hails taxicabs.

Conversion

Check out time at the Majestic isn't until 1 p.m., so you will have plenty of time to take a parting look at the National Cathedral. And, while circling around the plaza, think back to over 500 years ago and imagine sailing the high seas back to Spain.

The year was 1477. The place was a church in Seville. It was then and there that a Dominican priest by the name of Alonso de Hojeda addressed a congregation that included an exalted visitor, Queen Isabella. And, it was no run-of-the-mill sermon. Father Alonso convinced the Queen that some of her "converted" subjects were secretly practicing Judaism. The padre's preaching must have made quite an impression upon this very devout Queen because soon thereafter, she and her husband King Ferdinand launched Spain's version of the Inquisition to rid Spain of heretics and doubters of every variety, including Muslims and Jews. For that, the Pope was very grateful. And so it was that a very special relationship began between Spain and the Catholic Church.

In the decades to follow, the discoveries of strange and far-distant lands meant that there would be countless new souls in need of salvation. In 1492 the Pope mandated "New World" natives be instructed in Catholicism. But it wasn't just the Pope who thought that the natives had to be converted. The ground rules for dealing with Indians in Spain's colonies were laid down by King Ferdinand himself. By the "Law of Burgos" King Ferdinand decreed: "*WHEREAS, the King...and my Mother (may she rest in glory!) always desired that...the Indians...be brought to a knowledge of our Holy Catholic Faith....we ....command...that...*[the person(s) in charge of the Indians] *...teach them The Ten Commandments...---Also, we order and* *command that...the priests... say Masses on Sundays and obligatory feast days;---Also we ...command who ever has fifty or more Indians...to have a boy...taught to read and write... the things of faith, so that he may later teach the Indians....---Done in this City of Burgos, December 27,1512. THE KING...."*

The decree was Spain's first attempt to draft comprehensive laws to govern the natives. The law was sporadically enforced, and it applied only to some islands that became Spanish colonies. Still, the message about *faith* was unequivocal. The spirit of that law remained unaltered for centuries. The Holy Cross of Christ was soon to top steeples wherever Spanish troops could hoist the King's red flag.

Despite the edict's lofty rhetoric, however, the royal obsession with converting the Indians may have had little to do with saving souls. More likely, the King may have thought that armed invasions into new lands would be more palatable to the European continent if done for the sake of spreading Christianity.

There were other earthly considerations. Spain desperately needed cheap labor to do the hard work it would take to extract the riches of its colonies. The Crown knew that to endure slave-like conditions the Indians would need a set of beliefs that offered a better life in the hereafter. The Catholic faith filled that bill.

As for the Church, it had a public relations problem to deal with. Pope Alexander VI (1492-1503) had been an embarrassment to the papacy. Maybe memories of Alexander's mistresses and illegitimate children would fade if the faithful were told that the Church was spreading the word of Christ to the New World.

In short, there were a lot of reasons to force the natives to become Catholic.

Charles V assumed the Spanish throne in 1516. That was three years before Cortés landed on the shores of the land dominated by the Aztecs. Before setting sail, Cortés was under orders from the King to convert the Indians to Catholicism. Cortés took his orders very seriously. Thus, the Catholic Church got off to a roaring start in the New World. But, converting the Indians first required abandonment of native ways. At this, the Conquistadors excelled. They proved to be a lot better at smashing Indian idols and clearing the landscape of Indian ideology than they were at spreading the message of Jesus.

Even though the Conquistadors were anything but a pious lot, they had no stomach for the Indian practice of human sacrifice. Cortés and his men thought the practice was disgusting. Catholic rituals were somber, mystical, and orderly – a far cry from the ghoulish Aztec practice in which long parades of defeated enemies, numbering into thousands, trudged up the temple steps through the fog of burning incense, the beat of drums and the chants of priests. There the victims chests were split open; their beating hearts were torn from their bodies and offered to the gods; their corpses were then strewn down the pyramid steps, butchered, cooked, and eaten by Aztec warriors to nourish them for the next battle – all to be repeated time and time again. But there was more to these macabre shows than appeasing the gods. They were intended to terrify enemy noblemen and other invited guests so that they would think twice before waging war on the Aztecs. What the Aztecs didn't count on, however, was that it was just too much for even the Conquistadors. The Conquistadors put human sacrifice to an end. The work of the monks would follow.

Wave after wave of monks took over where the Conquistadors left off. Franciscan missionaries arrived first. The Dominicans followed. The Augustinians reached Mexico in 1533. The Jesuit order (Society of Jesus) came in 1571.

The monks built monasteries and convents. They taught the Indians concepts of Christian morality, preached to them about Mass, baptism, good and evil and heaven and hell. They translated confessional and religious writings into the Indian languages.

The monks' activities were not entirely in the evangelical spirit. The monks were granted authority to self-govern and they were awarded enormous parcels of land. Thomas More had recently written "Utopia," in which he portrayed a fictional community that reached toward perfection by use of discipline and structure. The Jesuits used the Utopian model to establish agricultural communities (called "reductions") to provide discipline over the Indians, tax them, administer to their needs, and, of course, to make them Christians.

Over time the monks became friends of the Indians. They learned the Indian languages. They built schools. The monks taught ceramics, masonry and other trade crafts to the Indians. They built thousands of churches which today form the core and center of every Mexican city and village. They protected the Indians from the excessive demands of the colonists.

Converting the Indians involved more than just letting "the light shine out of the darkness," to borrow from 2 Corinthians 4:6. There were other forces working in the Pope's favor, such as some striking similarities between the Catholic faith and Indian faiths. The Indians, too, had a heaven and hell and the hope of a life hereafter. They could make a connection between the symbolism of the wooden cross of Jesus and the Ceiba tree which was the ancient religious symbol of the Aztecs. And, the Catholic ritual of communion that involved partaking of the blood and body of Christ was not impossible for the Aztecs to fathom. They consumed flesh and blood in their own religious ceremonies.

A few other ingredients went into the conversion process. Long ago the religions of the world mastered the art of holding people in awe and obeisance. The Catholic Church in New Spain was no exception; it knew that clanging bells, burning incense, and lighted candles would win over the skeptics. And, the Indians were not unmindful that the Catholics took many holidays for themselves – just as the Indians did. It didn't take the Indians long to look forward to the feasting and fireworks of local feast days.

Still, if all else failed, there was the stick. The *audiencia* (court) knew how to deal with Indians who harbored doubts about abandoning their old gods. Someone could have asked Don Carlos de Texcoco about the hazards of worshipping Indian idols, but he was burned at the stake in 1531.[82] He was not the only one. By 1571, the Inquisition made its way across the Atlantic and that made a lot of believers out of wavering Aztecs. But even before the Inquisition reached Mexico, bishops had inquisitorial powers over those Indians believed to be engaged in idolatry.

Getting Indians to convert was one thing. Keeping them converted was another. Indians had a tendency to revert to their gods. The Crown eventually came around to believing that the death penalty was not the best way to enforce the Inquisition's maxim *"once a Catholic, always a Catholic."* So the King ordered that idolatry be handled by local priests, and he let it be known that "appropriate" punishments short of death (such as flogging) would suffice.

It all worked out as King Ferdinand decreed from the City of Burgos on December 27, 1512. Today nearly all Mexicans profess to being Catholic.

Exploitation

"Amen, amen I say unto thee, unless a man be born again of water and the Holy Ghost, he cannot enter into the kingdom of God" (John 3:1-21).

If that is true, the Indians should have thanked their lucky stars the Spanish forced the Indians to be baptized as Catholics. That is because most of the Indians were about to die. At the time of the Spanish Conquest there were about 20 million natives in Mexico – by 1600 barely one million remained.[83]

While there is disagreement among the experts about the numbers, every authority agrees that the sixteenth century was a demographic disaster for the native population of Mexico. The treatment of the Indians (including treatment of their children) working the plantations and the silver mines was unimaginable. Many of those who survived the work died of small pox, the plague, and other diseases imported from Spain.

You know about Hernán Cortés. You may not know about his arch rival named Beltrán Guzmán. As president of Mexico's first *audiencia,* Guzman planned to bring Cortés to trial for mistreating the Indians. He was hardly the one who should have been pointing fingers. "Bloody Guzmán," as he was known, and his troops went on a slaughtering rampage of their own. The Indians they didn't slaughter they tortured to find out where they could find silver and gold. Guzmán's atrocities landed him in a Spanish prison where he died, but that didn't deter others from following in his footsteps.

Torturing Indians had become the Spanish method of getting rich. Burning of feet, cutting off of hands, dumping Indians into spike-filled pits, depriving entire tribes of food and water, and cutting up body parts of dead Indians and feeding the parts to survivors was how the Spanish learned where the gold and silver were. Monks described these events to artists whose paintings and sketches made a lasting record of Spanish atrocities. Whole tribes could be hanged or burned to death. Infants would be fed to the Conquistadors' dogs. Stronger Indians were rounded up and hauled off to the mines as slaves.[84]

We have been to the mines of Zacatecas. The narrow tunnels spiral many layers into the mountains. Inside these dark caves Indian men, women, and children seldom saw the light of day. Those who didn't die in the tunnels that caved in, or who survived falling from rope bridges and rickety ladders, died from exhaustion or bad lungs. Life in the mines, if anyone can call it living, was unbearable.

In the end, exploitation of the Indians proved to be the only way there was for the Spanish to extract riches from its colony. But that harsh reality did not prevent some wishful thinking sparked by rumors of the fabled "Seven Cities of Gold." In 1539 Friar Marco de Niza, a Franciscan priest, reported to Spanish officials that he saw one of them – Cibola – in what is present day New Mexico. Acting on that tip, in 1540 the Viceroy sent out a search expedition led by his friend, Francisco Vázquez Coronado. Bloody Guzmán may have held the record for cruelty, but for being gullible the prize should probably go to Coronado and the 336 members of his party. Perhaps, on the other hand, there was reason for optimism; after all, the tip came from a priest; Spain had earlier recovered vast riches from the Incas of South America; the Aztec city of Tenochtitlan proved to be a rich and wondrous discovery. So why should Coronado and his men be "Doubting Thomases" about the Seven Cities of Gold?

They struck off on horseback with visions of fame and fortune. But the cloud of dust they left in their wake might just as well have been blowing in their faces. Everywhere they went native villagers would tell Coronado that the fabled cites were *más allá* (further on). The villagers must have been pointing northward because Coronado and his exhausted entourage got just about to present day Wichita, Kansas. That, of course, was 400 years before Wichita became the "Air Capital of the World." The only action around Wichita back then were roaming "shaggy cows" (buffalos). Coronado finally gave up. His men were angry and broke. The Viceroy was not pleased.

And the fabled cities of gold and wealth were never found because there were not any. The dismal truth was that exploiting the Indians was the only way to do what Spain wanted to be done.

Assimilation

Blending of the Cultures

*T*he story of the mistreatment of natives of Mexico has a counterpart in the United States. Neither country can take the high moral ground. If original intentions matter, it would be hard to make the case that the mandate from King James I to the Virginia Company – to find gold and a water route to the Orient – was any more, or less, altruistic than Charles V's expansionary intentions were with respect to New Spain. Neither King could claim to be more pious than the other. Intentions aside, the facts were different.

<u>In the United States</u>. The early settlors in the United States did not need the Indians to do their grunt work. They were not after Indian labor, they just wanted the Indians' land – so the Indians were pushed around, mostly westward. The survivors were herded onto reservations. Those herded on to reservations were the same people whose worship of the land was legendary. They were *"those who love sunshine on meadow— who love shadow of the forest—love the wind among the branches... the palisades of pine trees, the thunder in the mountains..."(*excerpts from *Song for Hiawatha)*.

When it became clear that there was not enough land to go around, the White Man and the Red Man concluded that they had to annihilate each other. It would be hard to say that Colonel John M. Chivington, a 19th century Methodist minister from Missouri, was more charitably inclined toward the Cheyenne Indians than Spain's Bloody Guzman was toward the Indians of Mexico. "The Fighting Parson," as Chivington was known, got the attention of his congregation with such openers as *"By the grace of God and these two revolvers, I am going to preach here today."*[85] And preach he did – but not for long in Missouri. To a gathering of deacons further west, he uttered these words: "*It simply is not possible for Indians to obey or even understand any treaty. I am fully satisfied, gentlemen, that to kill them is the only way we will have peace and quiet in Colorado.*" [86]

The Fighting Parson was not a voice in the wilderness. Chivington's animosity toward the Indians was shared by millions of U.S. citizens and had been baked into the interior policy of the United States. Shooting of warring Indians was within the rules of engagement. Genocide, possibly, it was not, but the massacre of the American natives is an ugly story many people have simply chosen to forget. Others remain unapologetic. Still others find comfort in saying that the United States, unlike Mexico, was settled by folks who had abandoned Europe and whose only intentions were to stake out farms and to worship their god under a government that allowed them to do so freely. Maybe so, but that would provide little solace for Hiawatha.

In Mexico. There was something going on in Mexico that was not going on in the United States – for the lack of a better word, that something was *assimilation*. By the time Benito Juárez, a full-blooded Indian, became president of Mexico in 1858, millions of Spanish whites had married Indian women and parented children of mixed blood. Mexicans of Spanish or Indian blood, and a combination of the two, ate the same food, liked the same music, went to the same churches, shopped in the same markets and dressed much alike.

It is probably fair to say that making comparisons can be futile. Both the U.S. and Mexico eventually realized they would have to admit their wrongs; in the United States Indians were recompensed with casinos, fishing rights, and so forth; in Mexico "wrongs" were "righted" with land redistribution, and so forth. But, in terms of assimilation of the native cultures, Mexico comes out on top.

There are many explanations why assimilation occurred. The most logical is that the Spanish had little choice in the matter. The Conquistadors did not bring women with them and there were problems on the European continent that kept many would-be colonists at home in Spain. Add to that, inter-marriage was encouraged by the Church. There are other explanations, but here is one that is a little less pragmatic:

Juan Diego was a simple Aztec peasant who, about five years after the Spanish Conquest, was baptized into the Catholic faith. The baptism must have gone well because six years later, on December 9, 1531, to be precise, he was visited by a vision of a brown-skinned Virgin Mary. (The monks' account of a white-skinned Virgin Mary was a difficult sell to the Aztecs. A brown-skinned version was more appealing to them.) The Virgin spoke

Virgin of Guadalupe

to Juan Diego in Juan's native Aztec language commanding him to set in motion the building of a Catholic Church at the very spot the two were talking. Juan pleaded the Virgin's cause to a puzzled bishop. Juan didn't win the bishop over the first time around. So Juan went back to the scene of the first appearance and encountered the Virgin again. There he was told to pick some Castilian roses, which did not grow in that part of Mexico. Miraculously, Juan Diego found Castilian roses, picked some, placed them on a cloak, and carried them back to the bishop as proof of the encounter. But the roses fell to the ground, and where the roses had been on the cloak there now appeared the image of the brown-skinned Virgin. All of this must have sifted back to the Pope. Eyeing an opportunity to win over the Indians, the Pope was quick to straighten out the doubting bishop. Soon the Church was built just as the Virgin directed. The Pope liked the story so much he assembled a truth commission to validate it. Sure enough – the miracle occurred exactly like Juan Diego described.

The story of Juan Diego's miraculous encounter spread like wild fire. The Virgin of Guadalupe is now worshipped in a new Basilica in Mexico City that accommodates some 10,000 people; images of the Virgin appear in countless churches, in homes, and in shops; replicas dangle from rear view mirrors of buses, trucks, and taxi cabs. Scented candles portraying the Virgin's image are stocked at nearly every market. December 12 of each year is the day of the Feast of Our Lady of Guadalupe. Millions of pilgrims come to the Basilica from miles away – on buses, on foot, and even on their knees.

No matter what one's faith or belief in miracles, it is widely accepted among scholars and skeptics alike that the Virgin of Guadalupe had a great deal to do with bringing together the Indian and Spanish cultures. On July 31, 2002, Pope John Paul II canonized Juan Diego at the new Basilica of Our Lady of Guadalupe. The Pope described the new saint as "a simple, humble Indian" who accepted Christianity without giving up his identity as an Indian.[87] Perhaps, as it has been said, God counted on Juan Diego to bring the Good News to the people of Mexico.[88]

That is one story about assimilation. Here is another – this one's a bit different.

Saint John the Baptist Church

There is a church in Mexico (one among many, perhaps) where the congregation has clung to many of its Indian ways. It is a small white church with folksy yellow and blue trim in the highlands of Chiapas, not far from the border with Guatemala. It is named Saint John the Baptist Church and it faces the central plaza of the village of San Juan Chamula, home to mostly Mayan descendants. We visited this church several years ago. Photos are not allowed inside the Church, so a description will have to do.

This is one remarkable place. There are no pews in this church. The floors are bare except for pine boughs and clusters of Mayan families in native dress, sitting or kneeling around candles, flowers, and Coca Cola bottles. They appear to be communicating with their spiritual world, or faith healing. Cokes and a brew called "pox" are offered to the saints for good health and good fortune – and to belch away evil spirits. We were told chickens, butchered on that very floor, are sacrificed for the same reasons. Dogs and cats are rumored to meet the same fate. Statues of the

Virgin of Guadalupe and of lesser saints stand in rows of vertical glass boxes peering at the rituals performed in their honor. The dim candle light, thick smoke, and smell of burning copal – layered upon the drone of chanting and murmurings – made us feel that we were entering into, and intruding upon, their ancient and sacred world. Maybe those huddled in worship were praying that we would go away.

One would not expect this to be a Catholic church. But the figure of Jesus, lying in a glass coffin, the cross on the belfry, and Catholic icons tucked into niches of interior walls, confirm that the Catholic Saints are in the right church. While Saint John the Baptist Church has no full-time priest, Catholic Mass is administered there on a regular basis to these reclusive heirs to the great Mayan culture.

A few skeptics wonder whether this small church in Chamula may be just a front for the Mayans to practice their ancient faith. Maybe so, but from our brief experience there, it seems these Mayans have "assimilated" the Catholic Church their own way.

Chiapas (1994)

*O*ne would think that the struggles of the Indians would be over by now. Wrong. Especially that was not the case in Chiapas during the waning years of the twentieth century. And it is not true now.

The beautiful mountains, valleys and jungles of the State of Chiapas border on Guatemala. The pearl of Chiapas is the city of San Cristóbal de Las Casas, nestled in the highlands where the air is cool and clear. The city is surrounded with villages of Mayan speaking Indians. It is named after a bishop who devoted his life to the cause of Indians. Persons wishing to know Mexico are well advised to entrench themselves for days in this wonderfully interesting and charming colonial city and probe the villages that surround it.

It is unlikely that anyone visiting there will chance on to a university-educated philosopher who wears a black ski mask (through which he smokes a pipe) and who goes by the name of Subcomandante Marcos, a/k/a Delegate Zero. The government of Mexico believes Marcos is Rafael Sebastián Gullén Vicente, born in 1967 to middle-class parents in Tampico, some 1200 kilometers north of where this story takes place.[89]

It is perhaps a contradiction to say that a masked man can be the face of a rebellion, but that is just what Subcomandante Marcos was – and is. While he is not a Mayan Indian, he took up their cause as if he were. The problems in Chiapas that outraged Marcos included Mayan homes with dirt floors, homes with no electricity, bad medicine and bad schools. These conditions caused Human Rights Watch/Americas to declare that "Chiapas has the worst socio-economic conditions in Mexico, a long history of agrarian conflict, and a record for injustice and human rights violations unparalleled anywhere else in the country."[90] As Marcos saw things in the

1970's and 1980's, these conditions were caused by fundamental injustices that had to be fixed. He also saw that it would take a rebellion to fix them.

Distribution of land has always lurked as an explosive issue in Mexico. Many years ago the *encomienda* system (see Chapter 9) paved the way for the Spanish colonists to grab Indian land and turn it into enormous haciendas and plantations. To keep the peace – and depending on the winds of politics – land was redistributed from time to time in the form of communal farm villages called *ejidos*. That is not to say that the redistribution was either adequate or fair, but in Chiapas and elsewhere *ejidos* had become a mainstay for many Indian peasants. Article 27 of the Mexican Constitution promised them that *ejido* land would not be sold nor exploited.

NAFTA

But things change, particularly in a global economy. In the early 1990s negotiations were underway between the United States, Mexico, and Canada to enter into a free trade agreement known as *NAFTA* (North American Free Trade Agreement). The treaty would essentially end tariffs between the three countries. Big-moneyed interests saw big opportunities and they placed their bets on *NAFTA* happening. Large Mexican cattle ranchers and coffee plantation owners began invading small chicken and pig farms, and loggers began bulldozing the jungle. The Mexican government turned a blind eye as President Carlos Salinas ducked the question whether anything government may do could save the small peasant farm. His choice, as he saw it, was either to save the small peasant farm or ratchet up Mexico's presence in the global economy. Mexico could not have it both ways.

Foreigners were reluctant to invest in Mexico's farms as long as Article

27 was on the books. They wanted Mexico's laws to be "modernized." Could not their investments be appropriated in such a "backward" country? So Article 27 was compromised. Now the treaty negotiators could put the finishing touches on NAFTA.

The small peasant farmers in Chiapas did not understand the fine points of the treaty but they knew that farming was all about yield. They knew too well that air-conditioned combines in America's heartland could swipe twelve rows of chemically-enhanced and genetically-modified corn with just one pass-through, and that peasant families hand-picking corn in Chiapas would be no match for the three-hundred bushels per acre standard to which U.S. growers strived.

Mexico is a country where only 12% of the land is arable.[91] Credit for small farmers is next to impossible to get. How could the peasants squeeze out of their tiny plots enough to compete in a world where bigger is better? So, while heads of three countries were congratulating each other for opening up trade in North America, the Mayans of Chiapas were talking about how to save their farms.

With the help of the local clergy, the Indians organized and formed credit unions; they developed methods of processing, and learned about marketing and improving trucking. And, they also retook some of their land. The land they took back did not go unnoticed by the landed gentry. They fought back with "white guard" private armies and there were bloody confrontations.

Marcos saw these events unfold from Mexico City's prestigious Autonomous University and, even though he was not Mayan, nor was he from Chiapas, he did not like what he saw. He knew all too well that the problems of the Indians had not been cured by prior revolutions, so Marcos planned another one. This one, he would lead.

When Marcos first met with the Mayans in Chiapas he is reported to have said that he felt like a creature from a different planet – a fitting observation given that he was talking to an audience of Mayans whose ancestors knew a great deal about the planets. But the Mayans saw Marcos as a savior with feet firmly planted on the ground they were determined to keep. He met with them often and planned a revolution that he would lead.

Marcos had a way with words – an art he learned from his school teacher parents – but just a few words set the stage for the Declaration of War he delivered from the Lancandon jungle on New Year's Day, 1994. "*YA BASTA!*" can be translated to "*ENOUGH IS ENOUGH!*" His stirring oration in the jungle that day recited centuries of abuse. It was a New Year's resolution of a very different kind and it started the new year with a bang. It was no coincidence that *NAFTA* became effective that very day.

The Mayans were ready to fight to their deaths but there were not enough rifles to go around. Those that had drawn short straws carried fake wooden guns.[92] Known as the Zapatistas (or EZLN), they captured four communities, seized ranches, freed prisoners, set fire to police buildings and military barracks. But the Zapatistas's 3000 troops were no match for the 15,000 troops, tanks, and helicopters the federal government dispatched to the region the next day. It all ended twelve days after it started. According to one source, the death toll of Indians was around one thousand.[93] Some were captured and bound before they were shot. Marcos and the remaining Zapatistas fled to the jungle.

The battle ended swiftly but the cause went on. The Zapatistas later developed a communications campaign using the internet, cellular phones, newspapers, and marches, all for the purpose of bringing non-violent pressure to bear on the government. Other Mexican and international groups became attracted to their cause.

Fifteen years after the uprising Harvard sponsored a conference to assess the effect of the rebellion.[94] The participants were puzzled why the plight of the peasant had changed so little. They were puzzled because the rebellion had, in fact, altered the political balance (at least at the state and local levels), and large amounts of land were redistributed to the poor. But the political balance remained skewed toward the top, the redistributed land was of poor quality, and it was divided into plots that were too small.

Life in Chiapas today may look normal, and there has been halting progress. Yet many of the indigenous poor continue to live in wood slat houses with dirt floors and drink dirty water. They have turned inward and have experimented with "autonomous zones of power" as a form of parallel government. The federal government in Mexico City keeps a watchful eye on those people whose hero is the man in the mask.

The plight of the Indians goes on to this day. But we have leaped ahead of the story and need to pick up where we left off, namely when the people of Mexico finally realized that they had had *"ENOUGH"* of Spain.

Independence (1821)

Miguel Hidalgo – Father of the Nation

The city of Guanajuato is sunk deep into a narrow highland valley in the center of Mexico. It is surrounded by mountains that once were veined with silver.

The name "Guanajuato" translates from the Indian language to "Place of the Frogs." Once upon a time, the Indians must have found a lot of frogs there. We can say for certain that the Spaniards found a whole lot of silver there. By the end of the eighteenth century the "Place of the Frogs" had become the largest producer of silver in the colony. Guanajuato is now a state capitol, a university town, a cultural center, and a photographer's delight. It was the birthplace of the renowned muralist, Diego Rivera, and it is where some of Mexico's most distinguished writers once lived.

There is only one main road into this steeply pitched city of some seventy thousand people – and there is only one main road out of it. And, they are different roads. One might think that one road in and one road out would make driving in and out easy. Not so. This book is pretty much devoid of travel tips, but here is one to remember: If you go to Guanajuato by car, drive around the outskirts until you find an idle taxi; hire the driver to lead you and your car to your hotel. Then, park your car and leave it parked.

The main street follows the original course of the Guanajuato River. Many of the streets are underground following old drainage ditches and abandoned mining tunnels. Maybe it's the tunnels that make travelers feel a bit queasy, but dark tunnels cannot hold a candle to the city's Mummy Museum. It seems that in the late 1800's the city was having a problem with some of the locals who didn't want to pay a special tax for the perpetual care of deceased loved-ones. So, the city exhumed those bodies and put them on display for anyone to gawk at who could part with the price of admission. It was an instant hit and is now a favorite tourist attraction.

That's enough of Guanajuato's dark side – there is light at the end of every tunnel. The sun shines brightly over Guanajuato's central plaza, *Jardín Unión*, where students, townspeople, and tourists mix comfortably with each other. The historic center is filled with colonial mansions, cafés, brightly colored homes and shaded plazas. The city is riddled with winding alleys many of which are not wide enough for even small cars. After the sun goes down, student singing groups *(estudiantinas)* parade with visitors through the city's cobblestone streets and alleys. Balconies hang over the narrow alleys, the most famous of which is *Callejón del Beso* (Alley of the Kiss). Locals tell that this alley is so narrow that lovers on opposite balconies can kiss each other. Another threadlike alley is named "*Sal Si Puedes*" ("Exit if You Can").

Exit? Anyone who can make it to the summit of Mount Everest is welcome to try. And, there are taxis for those who are not Sherpas. Otherwise, consider the tram. It leaves from the back of San Diego church that lies at the base of the city. The tram will take you high up to the rim of the city where a stone replica of a war hero, named *Pipila*, commands

Kevin Willert

Pipila and the Background of Independence

the best view in town. Pipila's real name was Juan José de los Reyes and the huge red-stone monument, known as *El Pipila,* honors his role in the Battle of Guanajuato – the first authentic battle on the long and bloody road to Independence.

Spain erred from day one. Instead of allowing New Spain to generate a viable and autonomous economy, it demanded that all manufactured items be imported from Spain. The silver and gold of the colony became a tug of war between the Crown pulling on one end and the upper crust of the caste system (see Chapter 9) pulling at the other end. Both acted as though the riches were inexhaustible. The Crown taxed everything from tobacco to gunpowder to finance its escapades on the European continent. The upper class hoarded what they didn't fritter away on lavish lifestyles.

Tension was the logical consequence of a caste system that enshrined false notions about the status of people. Criollos resented Peninsulares. Indians were little more than slaves. Even the clergy had problems as rifts developed between the secular clergy and the regular clergy.

The unquenchable hunger for silver and gold left the hills and forests of the colony denuded. New Spain was showing signs of becoming an ecological disaster. As early as the 1600's there were food shortages. The year 1785 was the "year of hunger."

All of the undercurrents bubbled during a time in world affairs when kings and castles were losing ground to constitutions and parliaments. Intellectuals were debunking the "Divine Right of Kings." People were rethinking old ideas about the authority of the King.

The King was not oblivious to his problems. In 1764 he sent troops to the New World to bolster the Crown's presence but that inflamed the Criollos and made matters worse. The Crown tried reorganizing the administration of the colony by creating posts that were only available to purebred Spaniards loyal to the King.

For some time King Charles III had been concerned about the rich and powerful monks in the Spanish colonies. They controlled schools, hospitals, and welfare, and had become a major economic and social institution in New Spain. Monks complaining about Spain's treatment of the Indians was nothing new, but the Jesuits developed other philosophical, political, and theological differences with the King. They went so far as to challenge the legitimacy of Charles III's right to be the King. To the King, the Church had become a state within a state and it was time to put the genie back in the bottle. In 1767 Charles III had the Jesuits rounded up – about 6000 in all – and sent off to Corsica. But, "pulling the rug out" from under the Jesuits just compounded the King's problems. The Indians had come to trust the clergy and looked to them for protection from the excesses of colonialism. It was no surprise, therefore, that the Indians saw a new reason to oppose the King and viewed the liberals as their natural ally. It was that alliance that made Independence possible. Expelling the Jesuits proved to be a royal blunder.

Evicting the Jesuits gave Independence another unexpected boost. The Criollos and the Jesuits had a history of not getting along with each other, so the King might well have thought that expelling the Jesuits would please the Criollos. The King was wrong again. The expulsion of the Jesuits was viewed by the Criollos as an act of intrusion into their world. Once the Jesuits were gone, the wrath that the Criollos had directed at the Jesuits was redirected to the Crown.

It was a bad time for the King to be fundraising in his colonies. But the King needed all the money he could get for his wars with Napoleon. To that end, Spain enacted the Act of Consolidation of 1804. Prior to the Act, the Church had lent enormous sums of money to New Spain's private economy, much of it to Criollo land owners. The Act required the Church to call in those loans – thereby freeing up capital to be lent to the Crown. This was not just pocket money; about one half of New Spain's capital was tied up in such loans. The calling in of these loans created a furor and caused many Criollos to lose everything they had. Those loans that were not repaid meant that the collateral securing the loans had to be auctioned off. Often the auctions brought prices less than the loan thus creating even more anti-Crown sentiment.

In 1808 and 1809 New Spain was revisited by droughts. Many could not afford corn. By 1810 there was a famine. In short, a lot was going on in New Spain that Spain should have paid more attention to – but Spain was preoccupied with its own problems. Napoleon had invaded Spain in 1808 and placed his brother Joseph on the throne. The future of Mexico hung in precarious balance.

The spirit of rebellion is vividly portrayed in José Clemente Orozco's famous mural of a white-haired priest brandishing a burning torch. *The Man of Fire* consumes the stairwell of the Government Palace in Guadalajara. This, as travel writer Terry Pindell aptly remarked, " is a dangerous painting." The name of that priest is Miguel Hidalgo, the "Father of the Nation."

Hidalgo was a priest, but not exactly what the Pope would consider to be a model Catholic. He didn't believe in the virgin birth or the infallibility of the Pope. In between his pastoral duties he found time for dancing and gambling. He fathered five illegitimate children. Rumors of his ways drifted to the Holy Office of the Inquisition which was supposed to put on public trial anyone who strayed from the Church. But nothing came of Hidalgo's unholy ways.

Hidalgo did not appear to be the type to lead a revolt. He was in his 50's; an established priest, an upper class citizen, and a property owner. But he was frustrated and angry. He was mad at Spain because the Consolidation Act deprived him of some of his rents. He was mad because he had been fired as rector of a college in Valladolid. (The rumor was that he was fired for embezzling funds to pay off gambling debts). He was mad over the way Indians were treated.

Hidalgo was not the only man of the cloth who was mad. These were times when few people could read or write. Folks got their news delivered from the pulpit on Sunday mornings and the sermons they listened to were anything but complimentary toward Spain's money-grabbing-ways. If there were royalists in the congregation, they were sleeping in the pews.

The fight for independence needed only a spark. At six o'clock on the morning of September 16, 1810, in the town of Dolores – not far from Guanajuato – the bells started ringing in a little church of which Father Hidalgo was the parish priest. Flanked by several supporters, Father Hidalgo shouted his famous call to rebellion known as *Grito de Dolores* (Shout of Dolores – for short, *El Grito*). Just what words he used is unclear, but the message was crystal clear – *Death to bad government, and death to the Gachupines* (Peninsulares) – this, from a Roman Catholic priest!

Hidalgo had a message that was to alter history, and he picked the perfect time to deliver it. *El Grito* swung open the floodgate to Independence. But his followers of peasants and miners were untrained, and Hidalgo knew nothing about the ways of warfare – he was a priest, not a general. His unruly mob, armed with axes and knives, looted and pillaged neighboring villages. They picked up recruits as they marched from village to village under the banner of the Virgin of Guadalupe. Some of their recruits were royal officers and soldiers who switched sides. Hidalgo's angry pack headed toward Guanajuato.

The people of Guanajuato had been forewarned. Many of the wealthy sought refuge in the public granary which was made of stone and thought to be impenetrable. They brought their silver and prized possessions with them, trusting that the Viceroy's soldiers could hold the rebels at bay. But, Father Hidalgo and his 20,000 to 50,000 [95] fuming men were clamoring to prove otherwise.

The rebels had trouble getting to and through the granary door – that is, until Pipila came along. (He is the one with the good view of Guanajuato;

and, by the way, *Pipila* translates into *hen turkey,* so nick-named because he had a pocked face and he walked with the gait of a turkey.) Pipila strapped a large flat stone to his back so that musket balls bounced off him like water off of a duck's back. He got to the wooden door, burned the door down, and the attackers rushed in. But that was just the start. They went on to burn and loot the city and massacre many of its citizens. At first, they seemed unstoppable. They marched on with visions of conquests to come, but there soon was dissension in the ranks. Not all of those wanting independence wanted to achieve it that way.

Hidalgo and his troops moved on to Mexico City where they were forced to retreat. Hidalgo then hoped to continue his fight in Guadalajara and Zacatecas, but he was captured on July 31, 1811. He was brought before the Holy Office of the Inquisition. The Inquisition turned Hidalgo over to the military where he met his fate at the firing squad. His decapitated head (along with the heads of three other insurgents) was mounted on a pole and hung on display at the Guanajuato granary – a reminder to anyone thinking of following in Hidalgo's rebellious foot prints.

While Hidalgo's head was shriveling at the granary, his cause was continued by another priest, José María Morelos Pavón. Unlike Hidalgo, Morelos had a trained army with guns and they won many battles. He had an ambitious platform of equal rights, curtailing the powers of the Church and the army, and breaking up oversized haciendas. He declared Independence in 1813, but the war with Spain was far from over. In 1815 Morelos was captured, convicted of treason, and sent to face the firing squad. The revolutionaries scattered to the mountains. Morelos is nevertheless considered a national hero to this day.

The Viceroy's army remained in control until a guerilla leader by the name of Vicente Guerrero led another revolt. The Viceroy picked a general by the name of Augustín de Iturbide to stamp out Guerrero and his revolutionaries, but the decision to select Iturbide was a fatal one. Instead of fighting Guerrro, Iturbide "turned coat" against the Viceroy. Iturbide and Guerrero cut a deal with each other known as *The Plan of Iguala.* Iturbide was to go into the history books as a traitor, but the deal he made with Guerrero was a game changer.

The *Plan of Iguala* was very different than Hidalgo's *El Grito.* The plan had the tone of a compromise between those wanting a monarchy and those opposing one. Instead of *"Death to the Government,"* the *Plan of Iguala* was respectful of the King. It called for a constitutional monarchy; it retained the monopoly of the Catholic Church; it made Peninsulares and Criollos equals. It hinted that the King of Spain would appoint the constitutional monarch – but therein lay the trap. How was the King to know that Iturbide would seize the Crown for his own head?

Iturbide based his calculations on the fact that New Spain was exhausted from fighting and the hope that the King had written off the colony as a lost cause. However he may have gauged the situation, Iturbide seized power and named himself *Emperor Augustín I.* Thus, Independence turned out to be a very different event from what Hidalgo envisioned. Instead of inaugurating a president of a new republic, Mexico crowned an emperor. After all of the bloodshed and chaos, when Independence finally did come – some 11 years after *El Grito* – it looked like old wine in a new bottle.

His Highness, Emperor Augustín I and his wife, Empress Ana María, set out to rule in royal splendor from their palace in Mexico City. The coronation was splendid and grand. Protocol required the respect a king is owed, like kissing of the hand and bending of the knee. Iturbide was fitted out for his coronation by none other than Napoleon's French designer. The streets were scoured and laid with flower petals. Flags were hung from the church towers. Two bishops blessed the royal couple with holy water and led them to their thrones. All that pageantry would have looked pretty disgusting to Father Hidalgo. Pipila would have been devastated.

The inscription under Pipila's statue quotes him as declaring that there would be other granaries to burn. Truer words were never spoken. That aside, Independence was a *fete accompli.*

Search for Direction

The Royal Years (1821-1823)

The Emperor's reign would be a short one. Iturbide had his hands full governing just his own back yard, say nothing of an empire that stretched into northern California, the present day southwestern United States, and into almost all of Central America. One by one Iturbide lost the support of leaders in the outer areas of his empire. Problems were on every front. Mexico's neighbor to the north, the United States, was reluctant to recognize Iturbide – President Monroe thought that Iturbide would not last. Monroe was right. Another problem Iturbide faced was that Spain was plotting to retake its lost colony. And Iturbide was in deep trouble at home: the Mexican economy was in shambles from the wars for Independence, the mines had been vacated, the haciendas had been pillaged, the price of food was going through the roof, and the government was running out of money and no one would lend it any.

Iturbide was forced to abdicate in 1823. Some say Iturbide was Mexico's version of George Washington. Not many folks in Mexico buy that line. Iturbide was a self-appointed monarch – and not a good one, at least Mexico's Congress did not think so. He was allowed to flee to Italy but was condemned to death if he ever set foot in Mexico again. Still, there were those who were not happy Iturbide was gone and they encouraged him to come back. Instead of listening to his few remaining cheerleaders, he should have reread the death clause in his pension plan. Maybe he didn't know about it. Either way, the lure of again donning the emperor's clothes was more than Iturbide could resist, so he did set foot in Mexico one more time. When he got off the boat with his wife and children (accompanied by a chaplain) he was promptly arrested, tried, and sent to the firing squad. His last words were uttered July 19, 1824: "I am a traitor, No." Maybe not – but it was too late to say so then.

The nation was frayed after the Iturbide fiasco.

The two frayed ends were the *centralists* and the *federalists*, often expressed, respectively, in terms of *conservatives* versus *liberals*. The conservatives could loosely be grouped as large landowners, the privileged minority, the army, and the Catholic Church. To them, a powerful leader, a powerful military, a powerful Church, and censorship were needed to maintain political, social, and moral order. They knew exactly what they wanted. The liberals knew exactly what they didn't want. Liberals distrusted power in the hands of the few; they resented the power and wealth of the Church; they were against the constraints on intellectual inquiry the Church imposed. The liberals also had some ideas about what they did want. They wanted power distributed among the citizenry and they wanted a shot at competing with those at the top. It was the polarization of these two positions, and the hostilities back and forth between them, that was to be the story of Mexico for decades to come. It festers to this day.

In 1824 Mexico's Congress called for presidential elections. A military hero by the name of Guadalupe Victoria was elected president. He set the tone of his presidency at his inauguration with the words: *"Independence will be reinforced with my blood and freedom will be lost with my life."* With that said, he set out to rebuild Mexico. The Constitution of 1824 was enacted during Victoria's presidency. It was generally a liberal document, except for a few provisions that clearly were not, namely: The Catholic Church retained its monopoly; the clergy and the military were immunized from civil law; the president was given extreme "emergency" powers. It was a start. At least Mexico had a *real* president and, albeit not perfect, a *real* constitution. His good efforts did much to redeem Mexico in the eyes of the world, but his words could not stop the infighting between liberals and conservatives. Victoria was reelected in 1828 to a second four-year term but a military coup was organized against him. The National Palace was shelled, Victoria's reelection was annulled, and a leader of the coup, Vicente Guerrero, took over as President.

President Guerrero had more than domestic problems. Spain launched an invasion of Mexico to get back its treasured former colony. At the new president's side a Napoleon "wannabe" emerged by the name of Santa Anna. Santa Anna, the self-styled "Napoleon of the West," met Spain's forces head-on, crushed them, and went on to become a national hero – a happening for which Mexico would pay a very dear price.

The Long Regime of Santa Anna (1833-1855)

In 1833 Santa Anna, was elected president in a landslide. The electorate at first thought they were electing another version of Father Hidalgo and instead got a Napoleon "wanna-be." Santa Anna was a military dictator disguised as a liberal. Only after being sworn in as president did it occur to him that Mexicans were not "ready" for democracy.

Santa Anna quickly became a very rich man. His land holdings approximated one half million acres.[96] His lust for power and fame knew no limits. His busts and statues popped up throughout Mexico's parks and public places. Everywhere he went he was preceded by a 21 gun salute. He had a lavish theatre named after him. He was to be addressed as "Most Serene Highness." He was not Pipila's kind of a guy, but he certainly knew how to survive. From his election in 1833 to the time he left office for the last time in 1855 he managed to be president, off and on again, for twenty-two years.

One would think with a record like that he needed an unusually good campaign staff. Not really. His astonishing ability to keep bouncing back had a lot to do with his war hero image. Maybe that image had something to do with stringing the ears of dead enemies to keep track of the number he killed. Or maybe it was the system of justice he imposed over those he captured: if, while blindfolded, they drew a white bean, they were jailed – but that was a lot better than being shot if they drew a black bean. The best vote-getter of them all, however, was digging up the leg he lost in a battle and parading the leg through the streets of the capitol city. The real leg has long since disappeared but its cork replacement can be viewed at the Illinois State Military Museum in Springfield.[97] Better get there soon if you want to see it – Mexico wants it back.

In the United States Santa Anna is disliked for his skirmishes with Texas. Mexicans, however, dislike him for losing the Mexican-American War, about half of Mexico's land, much of their self-esteem, and for bringing Mexico to the brink of financial ruin. Had Santa Anna won that war, the Dallas Cowboys might now be a Mexican soccer team and Utah's Tabernacle Choir might be singing Catholic hymns in Spanish. But the war is another story. (See Chapter 2) He knew his long run was over when he was confronted with an armed movement to oust him. The legacy of Santa Anna puts him in the running with Cortés as the least revered figure in Mexican history. In 1855 Santa Anna resigned and went into exile. With that, Mexico's version of Abraham Lincoln appeared on the scene.

The Reform Era Under Benito Juárez (1855-1872)

It is unlikely that Pipila could have possibly imagined that Benito Juárez, a pure-bred Indian, orphaned at age three, who could only speak his native Zapotec language until age thirteen, would go on to become a much-beloved five-term president of his country. Benito Juárez changed the course of Mexico's history.

Juárez was trained as a lawyer. He was a liberal activist and the law was "his sword and his shield." He became president for the first time in 1858. Before then, he was Minister of Justice and in that capacity caused laws to be enacted to reign in the power of the Church. Known as the "Reform Laws," they made the clergy subject to the same laws as everyone else, prohibited the Church from engaging in activities unrelated to its core purpose, regulated fees the clergy could charge for baptisms and funerals, put limits on the ringing of church bells, and outlawed the wearing of clerical vestments in public. It may be hard to understand how such "anti-church" laws could set off a civil war. But the Reform Laws cut to the chase of the issues that divided liberals from conservatives, and when such laws were embodied in the Constitution of 1857, those who clamored for war were not to be deprived.

Reform War (1858-1861). In 1858 the conservatives started the war when they took over the capitol city, dissolved Congress, and arrested Juárez. Juárez escaped and set up a competing government in Veracruz. The "Reform War" was to go on for three years. What a mess! The country was split and so were its people. At first the conservatives had the upper hand, but the tide turned and the liberals regained the capitol of Mexico City in 1861. Juárez retook the presidential chair and was confirmed as president that March.

The French Intervention (1861-1867) Mexico was exhausted from the Reform War and was smothered in debt to European nations. In an effort to conserve cash, Juárez put a two-year hold on foreign debt repayment. That proved to be a mistake – at least France thought so. The French were itching for a reason to invade Mexico anyway. Many Mexicans were egging the French on because they believed that Mexico needed a European nobleman to rule the country – here was the chance of a lifetime to restore a monarchy. French troops invaded Mexico in 1861 and seized control of Mexico City in 1863. With the backing of Napoleon III, Maximilian of Austria was installed as Emperor of Mexico. Maximilian's reign only lasted a few years, but it took an insurrection to put it to an end. The Emperor was executed by a firing squad in 1867. He asked his executioners that he not be shot in the face and he asked to be forgiven. He was shot in the face anyway. Whether anyone forgave the well-intentioned Maximilian is another matter. His empress, Carlota, fled to France where she went insane from grief.

With the ouster of France, Juárez returned to office faced with gargantuan challenges. He died at his presidential desk of a heart attack on July 18, 1872 – a very dark day for Pipila.

*The Modernization of Mexico Under "The Strong Man"
Porfirio Díaz (1872-1910)*

The French intervention was a set-back for Mexico but it was a boon for the career of a young military man by the name of Porfirio Díaz. His role in battling the French made him a national hero and paved the way for him to become president in 1876. The General had a flare for politics – Díaz refunded to the national treasury the pesos he didn't spend fighting Maximilian. Perhaps he did this to signal to the nation that he was a liberal like Juárez, but if that was his signal, it did not fool the people for long. Except for one four-year term, the "Strong Man" (as he was called) held on to the title of President until 1911 – nearly one-third of a century. The four years he didn't hold that title he filled it with one of his puppets.

Díaz is often described as a dictator. His expression *pan o palo* (bread or stick) meant that he paid his underlings well (the bread) – after all, "a dog with a bone doesn't bite," – but he imprisoned or executed (the stick) anyone who did not do things his way. Díaz deputized bandits as *rurales* to execute his management style. It was the mounted *rurales* in their silver buttoned gray uniforms that kept the peace per the Díaz dictate "Catch in the act, kill on the spot." Who was going to argue with that?

Díaz wanted Mexico to be industrialized and prosperous like the United States. Díaz lamented, *"Poor Mexico, so far from God and so close to the United States."* [98] (Or was he lamenting the land lost by the "divinely" inspired *Manifest Destiny?)* Whether he ever said those words at all or what he meant doesn't really matter. He knew that Mexico was regarded as a "backward country;" a country where firewood was strapped to the backs of burros and where chickens and dogs roamed dusty streets; where extended families lived in one room shacks with dirt floors, no electricity, no running water.

© Enrique Velázquez / Lic.courtesy of Belva y Enrique Velázquez Studio, Ajijic • www.mymexicoart.com

This also was a country where there had been a mind-boggling succession of presidents, interim presidents, provisional presidents, and let us not forget Iturbide and Maximilian – so throw in a few emperors. Added to that a good number of Mexico's heads of state had ended their careers facing a firing squad; luckier ones were exiled to retirement spots far distant from Mexico's sunny beaches. Put that kind of banana republic turmoil in a country where banditos lurked behind cactus plants and it was no wonder that would-be foreign investors in New York and Europe were reluctant to plunk their money into it.

But don't underestimate Díaz. He had bold plans to change Mexico's image. He knew he needed to loosen the grip foreign investors had on their wallets. So he surrounded himself with a circle of technical advisors known as the *científicos* – those that knew the *science* of governing. Their objective was economic development. Mexico's many other problems would have to wait. Their expensive tailored suits and handlebar mustaches allowed these gentlemen to fit right in at the private clubs and marble banks throughout the industrialized world. Foreign investors knew that Díaz had the big picture but that he was no micromanager. They knew that Don José Ives Limantour, Secretary of Finance, was clearly the kind of guy who could grapple with fortunes while counting every peso. The Guggenheim family, William Randolph Hearst, and other elite "yanquis" talked his language. So did Old World big money. They all looked forward to their sojourns to Mexico because Díaz made certain they were given the respect they deserved. Díaz had dictated that foreigners were presumed to be "right" unless Díaz personally decreed otherwise. With that kind of neighborliness, what deep-pocketed globetrotter could turn down an invitation to have a little fun "after hours?"

Soon foreign investment poured into Mexico. Miners returned to their tunnels; mile upon mile of railroad tracks began spiking through the landscape; oil rigs popped from the ground. Mexico was on the mend. It was joining the prospering economies of the world.

But the improved economic state of things carried a horrible price tag. "Democracy" in Díaz's Mexico was a farce. Distortions in wealth were staggering. The infant mortality and life expectancy rates were appalling. People went homeless. Díaz's "modernization" pushed land values up— way up. Land companies were out surveying and subdividing land they didn't own – small farmers who couldn't produce documents of title lost their land.

Life on the hacienda was good, but only if you were the *hacendado,* the person who owned it, or a member of his family. One would not think that "keeping up" with neighbors would make much of a difference to a hacienda owner whose spacious house lorded over a 40,000 acre plantation. How would they even know what their neighbors were up to? Never mind… these gentlefolks felt compelled to display their gentrified status by traveling abroad, stuffing their homes with European paintings and extravagant furnishings, and sending their kids off to exclusive foreign schools. One extended family took it over the top. The family founder, Don Luis Terrazas, a former governor, had become quite astute in the manipulation of Díaz's land laws. Under his savvy management the family went on to own some seven million acres of land, say nothing of investments in railroads, textile and sugar mills—and on and on.[99]

The plight of the rural peons was quite another story – essentially they were slaves. Pay on the haciendas, mines, and factories was rock bottom; working conditions were insufferable; payroll practices were dishonest; women workers were sexually violated.

Mexico's constitution called for the essentials of a democracy, but how could democracy exist under these circumstances? The answer, of course, was that democracy did not exist. So, the liberals set out on a mission to put meaning into the constitution. One of them was a scholar by the name of Molina Enriquez. He published a book that was to Mexico what Rousseau's *Contract Social* was to the French Revolution. And there were other key players. The Flores Magón brothers put out newsletters that were so damning of the Díaz regime the brothers were forced to flee Mexico and publish their letters from St. Louis, Missouri.

Discontent was bubbling. In June of 1906 a group of copper miners went on a violent strike, and about the same time textile workers followed the copper miners' lead. Díaz was no jellyfish. His swift and brutal response put an end to both strikes, but crushing the strikers only made matters worse. Many Mexicans sympathized with the strikers and most Mexicans became resentful of foreign investment of any kind. They believed that the money Díaz extracted from outside of Mexico was not only robbing Mexican workers, it was robbing Mexicans of Mexico.

While these and other rumblings of discontent were going on, two unusual events occurred. The first was the 1909 eruption of Mt. Colima. The second was Halley's Comet a year later. Pipila asks: Were these the omens calling for action? Many unschooled and bewildered peons thought so. These strange events did not faze Díaz or his learned *científicos* – they knew all about volcanoes and comets. But they didn't know that Díaz had another problem. Some months before either the Colima or Halley's Comet events, the Strong Man's tongue slipped while being interviewed by an American journalist. Díaz said he thought that Mexico was ready for a democracy and that he wouldn't run for president in 1910. Francisco Madero, a left-leaning member of a wealthy Mexican family, seized upon this utterance and authored a book explaining why the country had had enough of Díaz. The name of the book was *Presidential Succession of 1910*. Díaz did not like the book one bit. That was not all that festered away at Díaz – the real insult was that Madero was drawing huge crowds when he toured the country on the very trains Díaz brought to Mexico! Díaz figured it best to allow Madero to run against him anyway. No negative campaign ads were to come from the "Strong Man;" instead, Díaz had Madero arrested before the election on grounds of inciting riots. Díaz won the election "fair and square." After the votes were safely in and counted, Díaz freed Madero with restrictions which Madero was soon to breach.

For weeks the 80-year-old Díaz had been over-seeing preparations in Mexico City for a grand and glorious centennial celebration of

Independence Day – it had been 100 years since Hidalgo's *El Grito*. The city was polished and laden with flowers. Kings, dictators, and heads of state throughout the world were invited to white-tie and silk-hat gatherings and to marvel at the pageantry Díaz had arranged for them. Díaz was particularly anxious for his guests to behold the marble opera house then under construction and its magnificent glass curtain made by Tiffany.

As *The Strong Man* sat in the parade booth that September 16, 1910, he certainly must have suspected that countless Mexicans were longing for a Mexico without Díaz sitting in the presidential chair. But neither he nor his wife, Doña Carmelita, would likely have guessed that one year later they would be fleeing the country on a German steamship. Díaz had little time to savor the centennial jubilation. Alarming reports from the countryside gave him the first clue. Then in November Madero called for an uprising. The poor and disadvantaged had to make a choice. They could continue suffering or become revolutionaries. They assembled in small groups in the countryside and villages throughout Mexico. The small groups turned into crowds. All of them had heard of Madero. The message of his book was not lost even on those who could not read a word of the printed page. Tension was in air. The shooting began the following May. The lid was about to blow.

The Revolution (1910-1920)

It started as a revolt against Díaz, but it soon fragmented into pockets of guerilla warfare throughout Mexico. Historian Anita Brenner describes the guerillas this way: "They had no…generals, no strategy, no organization....Each leader gave his own battle orders...and in the battle, the boys were on their own." [100]

The rebels battled federal troops wherever they could find *federales* willing to fight. They shot Díaz's silver-buttoned *rurales*, stopped trains, seized villages, and looted haciendas. Two of the best known rebel leaders were Pancho Villa and Emiliano Zapata. There were others, and they were a mixed lot. Some of the rebels rebelled in the name of land reform; some rebelled for a better constitution; some rebelled against foreign ownership of Mexico's resources; some were simply looters and thrill-seekers. Women and children joined the ranks. The rebels formed strange alliances and sometimes fought each other. But they had two things in common – they were desperate and they wanted change. And, they all knew nothing would change until Díaz was gone. The smoldering had turned into a wild fire. The Revolution was underway. Díaz knew his time was up. He resigned in October of 1911 and fled the country. Always one for colorful language, he had this parting remark: "*Madero has unleashed a tiger, let's see if he can tame it.*" [101]

The story of the Revolution is complicated and confusing – but it is not ancient history. Many in Mexico today recollect a parent or grandparent recounting some of the more colorful events of the day, such as the bandit Pancho Villa and his gang of roughnecks seizing cities and looting trains in the north as they shouted "*Viva la Revolución*" ("Long Live the Revolution"); Emiliano Zapata and his recruits in the south shouting "*Tierra y Libertad*" ("Land and Liberty"); bi-planes bombing insurgents in the north; the United States sending a naval fleet and marines to Mexico to protect "American interests;" Villa and Zapata marching into Mexico City with 50,000 troops. Chaos reigned supreme and it was to continue for a decade.

Chaos was to plague the office of President during all of those tumultuous ten years. Francisco Madero, the one who started it all, entered the presidency in 1911 with high hopes and good intentions but he could not bring stability to Mexico. There was a coup and Madero was assassinated. Victoriano Huerta, a drunkard General left over from days of Díaz, became President in 1913, was ousted in 1914, and died in exile. Venustiano Carranza, who became President in 1917, was assassinated in his sleep in 1920. Being president during the Revolution was a dangerous job.

The Revolution's dimensions and the tolls it took were staggering. By the time the Revolution ended (historians generally agree it ended in 1920) over one million lives had been lost in battle.[102] Some say two million –

no one knows for sure because many died of disease. Any way you look at it, some five percent of all Mexicans perished in those ten years, and probably a lot more.[103] It would have been hard to find a family who had not lost a spouse, child, sibling, or close friend.

Some people say the Revolution never ended. Why it is called a revolution at all is worthy of question. The Merriam-Webster dictionary defines "revolution" [in context of government] as a "fundamental change in political organization....the overthrow or renunciation of one government or ruler and the substitution of another.... ." Thus, we ask: When the Mexican Revolution finally was "over," was there a *fundamental change?* Or did the Revolution just tinker with a system destined to replace one *despot* with another *despot?* Did the Revolution accomplish anything *at all?*

Some say it put an end to generals usurping power and then becoming dictators. Some credit the Revolution for the creation of a system that enabled political parties (albeit, dominated by just one party for the next seven decades). Some say the Revolution created a spirit of national pride. Most everyone agrees that it produced a constitution making it at least possible for conditions to get better. The Constitution of 1917 was patterned after the U.S. Constitution. It bestowed basic democratic rights to the people, including the right of labor to organize; it curtailed the power of the Church; it allowed the poor to reclaim their lands; it declared Mexico the owner of resources beneath the soil, most notably, oil.

While the Constitution of 1917 bestowed these and other rights, skeptics wondered if it was all cosmetic. We will leave it to Pipila, as he gazes over the city where he burned the granary door over a century earlier, to ponder whether there are yet more doors to burn.

Clips of Last 100 Years

$\mathcal{T}$he last century has produced a complex and modern Mexico. The *"what, why and how"* of the last 100 years will be left to scholars to piece together and put in historical context. The following simply represents a selection of important events. What they have in common is that they left indelible marks on the country.

After the Revolution – A Chance for Peace? Álvaro Obregón was elected President in 1920. His four-year term saw education, labor, and land reforms. It marked the first stable presidency since the Revolution began. The revolutionary leader in the south of Mexico, Emiliano Zapata, was dead; in the north, Pancho Villa had retired to a hacienda and become a gentleman farmer. Could peace and prosperity be on the horizon?

Peace? Afraid not – more problems ahead. Obregón had shaky relations with the United States. Warren Harding was then President of the United States and his pro-big business administration was fixated on protecting U.S oil interests in Mexico. Harding refused to recognize the Obregón regime unless Obregón agreed that Mexico would not expropriate foreign oil interests. The trade-off was made. Many Mexicans felt that Obregón had sold out his country. Unrest heightened. Pancho Villa threatened to come out of retirement and he might have had he not been assassinated after spending a night with a lady friend. (It has been suggested that Obregón helped arrange for the assassination.)[104] Another of Obregón's detractors was a military officer by the name of Lucio Blanco. Some believe that he had in mind leading a revolt against Obregón. Blanco was last seen alive at a party in June of 1922. The next day his body was found near the Rio Grande following a shootout with government agents. Sound like old times? Maybe. Yet, despite it all, Obregón filled out his four year term (1920-1924) without being shot or ousted – quite an accomplishment seeing that Mexico had not had a peaceful presidential transition like that in four decades. But, Mexicans praying for peace in this very Catholic country were to discover that their prayers were not to be answered anytime soon.

The Cristero War (1926-1929). Plutarco Calles, an avowed atheist, was elected President in 1924. And, through military connections and puppet presidents, he continued as *de facto* president through 1934. He ruled with preverbial "iron fists." The ten years Calles dictated the affairs of State (dubbed the "Maximito Period") are not fondly remembered except, perhaps, by the inhabitants of a border city in northwest Mexico near Calles' birthplace. The city's official name is *General Plutarco Elias Calles* (population 12,849), one of the few public honors bestowed upon Calles. But the city fathers appear to have forgotten Calles. The city goes by the name "Sonoyta."

The city may have forgotten about Calles, but the Vatican did not. On May 21, 2000, Pope John Paul II canonized a group of saints and martyrs who rallied behind the Church during the religious war that Calles caused. The war is known as the *Cristero War* (1926-1929).

Calles had been raised by an uncle who had a fanatical hatred of the Catholic Church. That hatred rubbed off on Calles. When he became President, Calles stepped up enforcement of the anti-church laws that had been on the books for years and he layered on more of them. Convinced that the *"hour of victory belongs to God,"* groups of devout Catholics rebelled. The *"hour"* may have arrived for the rebels, but Calles didn't think that *"hour"* had arrived. He took the advice of a commander who said that squelching the rebels would be more of a "hunt" than a war. *Some hunt!* In Our Lady of Guadalupe Church in Guadalajara armed Catholics got in a shootout with federal troops. The Catholics surrendered when they ran out of ammunition, but not until 18 people were killed and 40 injured. The next day 240 federal soldiers stormed the church and, for good measure, killed the parish priest and his vicar. Neither side could claim the high moral ground. Catholic guerillas burned secular schools and murdered its teachers to the cry of *"Viva Cristo Rey"* ("Long live Christ the King"). For every teacher murdered, the government tried to kill a priest. The Cristero War went on for three years. About 90,000 people on both sides died in the war.[105] The "hunt" didn't look like peace from what Pipila could see. But Calles had a plan to bring peace and prosperity to Mexico.

The PRI. As powerful as Calles was, he could not legally be president more than once. Mexico had learned its lesson from too many years of Santa Anna and Díaz. So Calles created the political party that would later become the Institutional Revolutionary Party ("PRI"). It was to be his way of hanging on.

Ostensibly, the idea behind the party was to institutionalize the Revolution by drawing together unions, peasants, and populist sectors of the country. Many people think Calles brought these groups together to consolidate his own power. After his four-year term was over in 1928, Calles began hand-picking successive presidents. He pulled that off successfully until 1934. But Calles calling the shots came to a screeching halt in that year when he realized, to his dismay, that he would not be able to manipulate the party's next choice – Lázaro Cárdenas. A "yes man" Cárdenas was not.

The Cárdenas Years (1934-1940). Cárdenas meant business about returning the party to its revolutionary heritage. He started his administration by rounding up Calles and his cronies and arresting or deporting them. Cárdenas was devoted to the cause of social reform. Historians describe him as a pensive man – he listened more than he talked. He especially listened to workers and peasants. An often repeated story[106] is that, one day, his secretary presented Cárdenas with a stack of papers dealing with one crisis after another. The first dealt with money matters. Cárdenas instructed his secretary **"Tell the Treasurer."** He was told agriculture production was falling – **"Tell the Minister of Agriculture."** Then he was told there were new problems with the United States **"Tell Foreign Affairs."** The list of urgent events went on and on until Cárdenas read this telegram from a peasant: *"My corn dried, my burro died, my sow was stolen, my baby is sick. Signed: Pedro Juan, village of Huitzliptuzco."* **"Order the presidential train. We leave for Huitzliptuzco at once."**

Not everyone believes that story, but most people believe that Cárdenas was a caring person. He was not religious, however. He said that "man should not put his hope in the supernatural – that every moment spent on one's knees is a moment stolen from humanity."[107] His world consisted of fixing things that he could fix. Presidents before Cárdenas talked about land redistribution and some acted on it. However, Cárdenas was responsible for redistributing more land to communal farms (*ejidos)* than all of his predecessors combined – some 49,000,000 acres in all.[108] Government-sponsored schools and hospitals were incorporated into the *ejido* communities. *Banco de Crédito Ejidal* was set up to make loans to the *ejidos.* But that is not all Cárdenas did. He built roads and nationalized the nation's oil industry. (More about oil at Chapter 22) He was a staunch supporter of education (he allocated more money to education than all his predecessors combined). He built modern secular schools. He supported workers' cooperatives to counter the excesses of big business. He put an end to capital punishment.

The contrast between Calles and Cárdenas was stark. So too would be the policies, philosophies and personalities of the PRI presidents to come. But the PRI proved to be a strong and enduring institution in a country that desperately needed stability. Mario Vargas Llosa is a Peruvian writer who won the 2010 Nobel Prize in Literature for his works on Latin America. In 1990 Llosa referred to the PRI as "the perfect dictatorship,"[109] presumably referring to the way the PRI kept "tight control of public life."[110] Elections in the year 2000 put that assessment in doubt. In that year Vicente Fox, a Coca Cola executive and the National Action Party (PAN) candidate, became president. In 2006 Felipe Calderón, also from PAN, assumed the presidency. But in 2012 the PRI bounced back with the election of PRI's Enrique Peña Nieto. So the PRI may be the "perfect dictatorship" after all – time will tell. Either way, Pipila would have to admit that the PRI provided the stability the nation needed to move forward.

World War II (1939-1945). Return now to the build-up of World War II.

It was far from clear that Mexico would side with the United States. Who ever said that bordering neighbors had to be allies? Who in Mexico could forget that the United States invaded Mexico less than 100 years earlier in a land grab? And what about the U.S. boycott of Mexican oil? Why not sell that oil to Hitler? Sentiment was not just about settling old grudges, however. More than a few Mexicans were drawn to ideals of fascism. They watched the saga of Hitler unfold in Germany and Nazi propaganda found its way into Mexican newspapers. They witnessed Spain's Civil War and some were attracted to dictator Franco in Spain.

President Franklin Delano Roosevelt was nervous about Mexico's waffling. His Vice president-elect, Henry Wallace, started diplomatic talks with Mexico's next president, Manuel Ávila Camacho. The talks paved the way for an oil agreement in 1941, but it took German submarines torpedoing Mexican oil boats in 1942 for Mexico to quit sitting on the fence. Mexico declared war on the Axis Powers, furnished goods and materials to the war Allied effort, and provided an air squadron known as the Aztec Eagles that fought in the Philippines. Countless Mexicans living in the U.S. fought with the U.S. military. So, despite the doubts the U.S. initially harbored, Mexico turned out to be our good friend in the war.

The Economic Miracle (1930-1970). The period from 1930 to 1970 is known as Mexico's "Economic Miracle." Annual growth of 3%-4% was brought about by government polices of high tariffs on imported goods, investing heavily in railroads, energy, and infrastructure. Education enrollment tripled between 1929 and 1949. The war helped the miracle as did the policies of many PRI presidents.

Labeling this a "Miracle" may seem like a reach in the biblical sense of the word, but this was a country with a turbulent past that seemed to take two steps back for every step forward. Could Mexico ever become a prospering nation of the world? The "Economic Miracle" proved that it could. But, by 1970 the "Economic Miracle" of Mexico was looking like a mirage. Mexico had borrowed excessively from abroad and was suffering from unbridled inflation. The peso was allowed to float, but it sank like a rock. Charges of corruption and cronyism swirled around *Los Pinos* (Mexico's version of the White House).

The miracle had not ended, however; it simply took a breather. Despite the drug war and "Great Recession" that began about 2008, the economy of Mexico came roaring back. Mexico is now booming.

The Communist Threat in Mexico. Dwight D. Eisenhower was president of the United States when Aldolfo López Mateos took office as President of Mexico in 1958. By then, Wisconsin Senator McCarthy was disgraced and dead, but his ghost lived on. Eisenhower was consumed with the world-wide Communist threat, including in South and Central America and in Mexico. He had reason to be concerned about Mexico. Just three years before Mateos became president, President-dictator of Cuba, Fulgencio Batista, freed some political prisoners. Among those set free were Fidel Castro and his brother, Raúl. Once freed, they headed for Mexico where they plotted with "Che" Guevara to take over Cuba. Their band of rebels left by a small boat from the shores of Mexico in 1956 and became guerilla warriors in the mountains of Cuba. In 1959 the rebels toppled the Batista regime. Batista fled to Florida with fortunes he had looted from Cuba's coffers. Fidel Castro got cozy with Khrushchev. John F. Kennedy was inaugurated president in 1961 and he, like Eisenhower, was very worried by the spread of Cuban-style Communism, including its spread in Mexico.

Former Mexican president Lázaro Cárdenas was still very much alive and active. In his retirement he had become a cheerleader for the revolution in Cuba. President Mateos got caught in the middle of some very delicate negotiations with JFK, on the one hand, the PRI on the other. To the frustration of Kennedy, Mateos chose a policy of non–intervention in Cuba, refused to condemn the Castro regime, did not endorse U.S. sanctions against Cuba, and maintained diplomatic relations with Cuba. But, Mateos did not want to throw the baby out with the bath water. To the great relief of the United States, Mateos distanced the PRI from its left faction. The PRI went on to select Gustavo Díaz Ordaz as Mexico's next president. (1964-1970).

President Ordaz was a no-nonsense authoritarian. He was also not very handsome – even Ordaz thought he was ugly. Someone once said of Ordaz that he was two-faced. He remarked to Lyndon Johnson: "If I had another face, do you think I would go around wearing this one?"[111] But his ugliness was nowhere near as ugly as the night of October 2, 1968.

The Night of October 2, 1968. It was during Ordaz's tenure that the *"Tlatelolco Incident"* occurred (Mexico's "Kent State" on steroids). Most people thought it was more of a massacre than an incident, but there opinions vary. Where opinions do not vary is that it became a world-wide public relations disaster for the PRI.

Plaza de las Tres Culturas is a plaza in the *Tlatelolco* section of Mexico City. Mexico had just invested enormous sums in preparation for the 1968 Olympics that were to be hosted in Mexico City. President Ordaz was in his fourth year of his six-year term. He was determined to keep the peace and Ordaz was a guy you didn't mess with. An organization of student protestors from many universities and schools throughout Mexico sought to use the Olympics as a platform for their causes. Maybe they should have realized that Ordaz had a reputation dealing with dissenters – his way.

On *La Noche de Tlatelolco* (the Night of Tlatelolco) thousands of students gathered in the *Plaza de las Tres Culturas* when helicopters appeared over the plaza, tanks and thousands of soldiers surrounded the plaza, and flares were fired. Which side fired the first gun is disputed. The police blame shots fired from nearby buildings. Many folks don't buy that explanation. Either way, knowledgeable estimates of students and bystanders killed reach into the hundreds.[112] Official government statistics admitted deaths in the mid-forties.[113] Not everyone agrees on the number killed, beaten, or arrested, but most everyone accepts that "The Night of Tlatelolco" was not a good night for the PRI.

The Night the System Crashed. The PRI would be in for more bad nights. Another one happened July 6, 1988. Mexico had flocked to the polls earlier in the day to decide a presidential race between the son of former President Lázaro Cárdenas, Cuauhtémoc, and Carlos Salinas, who had earned a Ph.D from Harvard ten years earlier. Salinas was the PRI candidate. It looked like a tight race.

The PRI wasn't used to tight races; in fact, it had never lost a presidential election. And it didn't lose this one either. When the polls closed that evening the government started tallying the count at its central computing office. The next morning the Minister of the Interior announced "*se cayó el sistema*" ("the system crashed") and that the election results would be delayed. A week later Salinas was declared the winner by a wide margin and he went on to serve his six-year term. Ex-President Miguel de Madrid didn't stay on script when years later he inferred that Cuauhtémoc had really won the election, but that off-hand remark was chalked off as a "senior moment." Many contend that Salinas would have won even with a recount. No one knows—or ever will know. The records were destroyed. In that same election the PRI came close to losing majority status in the Chamber of Deputies and the PRI lost some seats in the Senate.

Another bad night for the PRI began at 7:12 PM on March 23, 1994. At that moment, Donaldo Colosio, the PRI's pick for the 2000 presidential election was shot in the head at a campaign rally in Tijuana. Conspiracy theories never died despite a special prosecutor's finding that Colosio was killed by a lone gunman. One such theory is that a faction within the PRI had him killed because he wanted to rein in its power and perks.[114]

Cronyism and Corruption – A Timeless Problem. Examples abound – as they do in every country. Here are a few Mexican examples.

PRI's José López Portillo became President in 1976. He left behind the worst economic mess Mexico had experienced in modern times. Portillo was the President who said he would defend the peso "like a dog."[115] He must have been referring to a Chihuahua. People barked at him when he retired to his lavish and newly built compound dubbed "Dog Hill," paid for with "inexplicable wealth" he somehow managed to accumulate while on the public payroll. Shortly before his death, Portillo was quoted as saying: "I do not enjoy perfect health, perhaps I'm paying for my sins."[116] He was not given a state funeral.

In contrast, the 47-year-old Harvard-educated Miguel de la Madrid (1982-1988) took the presidential office next. He had made corruption a major part of his platform, and he stuck to his word. He saw to it that a former director of PEMEX (Mexico's national oil company) served a long prison sentence for absconding with $43 million;[117] Mexico City's police chief (and good friend of former president López Portillo) was similarly destined to spend years behind bars.[118] He purportedly had some $600 million stashed away in foreign banks – not bad, on a police chief's salary.[119]

Next up as President after Madrid was Carlos Salinas (1988-1994). He had some troublesome distractions due to his brother, Raúl. It seemed that Raúl may have amassed a sizable fortune while Carlos Salinas was president – at least, eye brows were raised when hefty Citibank accounts in foreign branches popped up that were linked to Raúl.[120] The Swiss authorities thought it curious that a mid-level public servant might have accounts hovering around the 100 million dollar mark. Raúl claimed the money was just entrusted to him for safe keeping.[121] However, one report claims that a good portion of the funds was ultimately repatriated to Mexico.[122] None of the shenanigans alleged against Raúl connected President Salinas with evidence of wrongdoing.

What's Ahead? It would take many more clips to tell the stories of the last one hundred years. They would be of good times and bad times and of sunshine and rain. An old Mexican proverb says: *No hay mal que por bien no venga* (There is no bad from which good does not come). Whether Mexico has had more than its share of bad times begs the question—it has had plenty. But there is a rainbow over those same clouds.

Mexico has been blessed with many enlightened figures in politics, business, religion, literature, and art – in short, in every aspect of its culture. The people of Mexico have overwhelmingly followed with steady hands, high hopes, respect for the moment, and faith in the future. All paid off.

Today Mexico is the 13th largest economy in the world.[123] It has rapidly developing industrial and service sectors. It has made massive strides toward improving its infrastructure of toll roads, bridges, railroads, and electric output. It has trade agreements with 44 countries.[124] It has a labor force of 78 million workers who, by at least one measure, are the hardest working on the planet.[125] Other people of the world must see the good side of Mexico too. It is the tenth most visited country in the world.[126] Pipila would be pleased. He would have reason to be.

Death

Kevin Willert

Catrina Doll – A Joking Matter

Nadie se va de este mundo vivo. (No one leaves this world alive). Mexico can hardly be credited with being the country of origin of something so obvious. Yet, Mexicans can be credited for recognizing that dreading death is not the only way to think about it. Octavio Paz (a Mexican writer and winner of the 1990 Nobel prize for literature) wrote: "the Mexican is familiar with death, jokes about it,…celebrates it…. Our songs, proverbs, fiestas and popular beliefs show very clearly that the reason death cannot frighten us is that life has cured us of fear." [127]

Nowhere can this better be witnessed than during *Día de los Muertos* (Day of the Dead). It sounds like a one day event. Actually, celebrations go on for two days (November 1 and 2). November 1 is All Saints' Day and November 2 is Day of the Dead – but for celebrating purposes, the two have been rolled into one. (Two days is a flash in the pan compared to the Aztec celebration of death that went on for an entire Aztec month.) There is nothing funereal about the Day of the Dead celebrations. Entire families spend long hours picnicking and socializing at the cemeteries of deceased family members whose graves they decorate with flowers and candles. Toys and candles are placed by the graves of deceased children. Favorite foods and drinks of the deceased are shared by loved ones. And, it is not just about sorrow for lost loved ones; the celebration is to draw

113

out the souls of the deceased and for the souls to mingle with the living. Tequila and other drinks are offered to the souls of the departed. Pillows and blankets are set out so that the souls can rest after their long journey to the grave site. Not all Day of the Dead festivities are in cemeteries. Altars are erected in homes with miniature colored lights, framed photos of the dead, and more flowers and candles.

Day of the Dead celebrations are said to be traceable, in part, to European origins. But, the Aztec influence is inescapable. The Aztecs mocked death and appeared to welcome it. To them, death was the continuation of life, not the end of life.

The Aztecs had many gods. One of them was *Mictlantecuhtl,* who, with his wife, *Micteacachuatl,* presided over *Mictlan,* the Aztec version of hell. When an Aztec died, whether the deceased went to hell or not depended upon how that person died, not upon how he or she lived. Dying a heroic death pleased the gods more than dying from old age.

The Aztecs carved stone statues of their lord of death. Mictlantecuhtl was variously shown to have a skull head, a necklace of eyeballs, and his innards protruding from his rib cage. Some scholars claim that this was not intended to be macabre but was meant to represent life, death and resurrection. Maybe so, but it may have been more mockery than anything spiritual or philosophical.

There is light-heartedness in Aztec death mythology. According to their legends, Mictlan served as a warehouse for the bones of dead Aztecs. Two other Aztec gods tried smuggling the bones out of Mictlan but dropped them while trying to escape. They had trouble putting the scattered bones back together, and that is why Aztec people are different from one another.

The Conquistadors had some whoppers of their own, but their view of death was no joking matter. To them death was terrifying, and that is why they clung to Christ's promise of salvation as the way death can be avoided. The Conquistadors tried to make the Aztecs fearful of death, but little of the Conquistadors' dread rubbed off on the Aztecs, and even less can be seen at Day of the Dead celebrations.

While Mexicans may sometimes joke about death, there exists a fringe cult that nobody jokes about. Nobody jokes about the two million or so followers of *Santa Muerte,* the Saint of the Dead. (For the record, the Catholic Church has declared that there is no such saint.)

Santa Muerte – Not a Joking Matter

Worshippers of Santa Muerte are found where desperate people are found, particularly in impoverished neighborhoods and in prisons. Santa Muerte followers are frequently linked to crime, whether they are criminals, victims of criminals, or simply are surrounded by criminals. Some glorify crime. The cult's followers are largely Catholic but Santa Muerte worshipers will find no altars to their Saint of Death in any Catholic church. The Church is particularly offended by the attempt to confuse Santa Murete with the Virgin of Guadalupe.

Altars to Santa Muerte can be found in homes or along highways. The police call them "narco-altars" and they have found Santa Muerte chapels deep in the mansions of drug lords. Santa Muerte altars are disturbing to the eye. Her figurine is often encased in a glass box. Her shrines come in many forms but what they have in common is a hooded female skeleton with a menacing smile; her bone hands extend from the sleeves of her long robe. She holds a sickle in one hand to remind everyone of the long reach of death. In her other hand she sometimes clutches a globe signifying her dominion over the world. Interpretations of the meanings of the sickle and globe vary, but the message understood by all is the universality of death – and, its inevitability.

The altars are decorated with color-coded flowers and candles. Green is for help with legal problems; red is for love and passion; yellow for healing diseases; black for protection. Each color at the altar has a separate meaning.

Those faithful to Santa Muerte are blunt and specific in what they ask her for: help me get out of jail; protect me from the police; make me rich;

ruin my enemy – and so the wish list goes. Her worshipers seek protection and favors, not spiritual peace.

Santa Muerte does not bestow favors for free; she expects to be paid for them. Her practitioners place cigarettes, candy, tequila, and fresh flowers (plastic flowers do not please her) at the foot of her altars. The air around her statue is purified with cigar smoke.

The greatest concentration of Santa Muerte followers is in the impoverished neighborhood of Tepico, in Mexico City. There a self-appointed archbishop presides over midnight masses. Some in attendance are teen-agers clad in spooky cult garb; many are seemingly ordinary people who feel their petitions for help are not answered by Catholic saints. Santa Muerte does not lecture to them about the consequences of sin because all people are sinners. Everyone is welcome because everyone dies.

Many Santa Muerte believers have a look of their own. They wear Santa Muerte jewelry and T shirts, and their arms, backs, breasts, and butts are tattooed with her image. But others could fit right in at a Methodist church in Kansas.

The case is made that present day followers of the cult seek to form a linkage with the Aztec past. Some claim linkage to Europe, Guatemala, or Africa. Wherever or whatever the linkage may or may not be, the cult is not old. Practitioners can only be traced back about 50 years, but its numbers are growing. It has crossed the U.S. border and its images can be found on candles, necklaces, and junk merchandise just about everywhere.

Despite the growth of the Santa Muerte cult, its adherents account for a very small part of Mexico's population. Its growth among the desperately poor probably is tied to economic times. Better times are apt to reverse the trend.

Nonetheless, Mexico's fascination with death flourishes – in its many fascinating forms.

Holidays

Mexico is in a perpetual state of celebrating one event or another. At least, it seems that way. Some celebrations are unique to Mexico's national heritage; others are religious and transcend national borders, although they can take on regional and local characteristics. Here are a few that are special in the way they are celebrated in Mexico, or that have exceptional stories behind them, or both.

Aniversario de la Constitución (Independence Day) – September 16. Think back to Mexico City's Hotel Majestic on the *Plaza de la Constitución* (Chapter 9). It's the day before Independence Day and you are looking out at the National Palace while sipping a late-night beer at the roof-top bar. The plaza is lined with green, white, and red lights. It is a sea of patriotic men, women, and children fluttering hand-held flags. At 11 o'clock Mexico's President, standing on the central balcony of the palace, rings the palace bell, shouts words of *El Grito,* and yells *"¡Viva México! – ¡Viva México! –¡Viva México!"* Fireworks explode. Confetti rains down upon the cheering crowd. What a sight! The next day, September 16, the country takes the day off in gratitude of Independence – a reward that was duly earned after three centuries of Spanish domination and a decade of fighting to free itself.

Los Niños Héroes (The Hero Children) – September 13. In 1847 some 12,000 U.S. troops landed in an amphibious assault of Mexico's port city of Veracruz. Winfield Scott was in command. Among those in the invading party were Robert E. Lee, "Stonewall" Jackson, and Ulysses S. Grant. This was the U.S. invasion into Mexico's heartland in what became the Mexican-American War. (Chapter 2). Veracruz surrendered after twelve days of fighting. On the floor of the U.S. Senate, Abraham Lincoln and John Quincy Adams described the invasion as unjust. The noted essayist, lecturer, and poet Ralph Waldo Emerson joined the chorus of dissenters. But those voices were drowned by the expansionists who believed in the Manifest Destiny.

From Veracruz the U.S. troops went on to the city of Puebla. Puebla capitulated. Then it was on to Mexico City and the Battle of Chapultepec. It was that battle that put the final chapter on the Mexican-American War. Chapultepec Castle was then a fort that guarded the entrance to Mexico City. It also served as a military academy for cadets. Mexican troops were greatly outnumbered as Scott's troops stormed the castle with ladders. Mexico's General Nicolás Bravo ordered that his men retreat, including the military cadets in training. Six teenage cadets, ranging from 13 to 19 years of age, chose to stand their ground. All six were killed. One is said to have wrapped himself in a Mexican flag before he leapt to his death. A huge monument now stands at the entrance to Chapultepec Park in their honor. Streets are named after them and their images appear on Mexican currency.Every September 13 the nation pays tribute to *Los Niños Héroes*. It is curious that a monument of this prominence and a holiday of this significance would be dedicated to a battle that Mexico lost and that, ultimately, led to the loss of much of her territory.

Cinco de Mayo (The Fifth of May) – May 5. Chapter 15 recounts another war Mexico lost – the war with France. But the celebration every fifth day of May is remembered for a battle of that war that Mexico won. After President Juárez was forced to default on payment of foreign debt, including funds owed to France, France responded by landing troops on Mexico's shores. Some 6000 well-armed French troops marched to Puebla de los Ángeles, a small town in east-central Mexico, where they attacked half that many Mexican troops. The battle began at daybreak; by sunset the French retreated. Mexico's victory amazed Mexicans more than it did the French. This battle would not end the war, however. France went on to defeat Mexico and in 1864 installed Maximilian as Emperor. So the old adage applied: Mexico won the battle but lost the war. But that is not how Mexicans saw it. *Cinco de Mayo* inspired pride and patriotism and it stiffened the Mexican resolve. In a space of about three years after Maximilian's coronation, the Mexican army drove the French army out of Mexico City and Maximilian was sent to the firing squad.

La Expropiación Petrolera (The Expropriation of Oil) – March 18. Chapter 22 describes the prize found beneath Mexico's soil – oil – and how the U.S. and Anglo-Dutch interests stole it from Mexico. This particular holiday celebrates the radio announcement in 1938 by President Cárdenas that he stole it back. He told the country before he told his own cabinet. The country went wild with excitement. Within months PEMEX was created to give it exclusive rights over extraction, refinery, and commercialization of oil. PEMEX remains a source of enormous pride to the Mexican people. From time to time proposals surface to privatize Mexico's oil – a very unpopular idea to most Mexicans.

Día de la Revolución (Revolution Day) – November 20. Revolution Day honors the Revolution of 1910. (Chapter15) Just how November 20 became the official day is somewhat hazy.On November 20, 1910, Madero had arranged to meet with his uncle to launch an attack that would start the Revolution. The uncle was to bring 400 men, but he showed up late with just ten men, thus delaying the start of the Revolution by 45 days. *When* it started is probably unimportant. *What* the Revolution accomplished, other than to oust Porfirio Díaz and usher in ten years of chaos, is debated to this day. Some critics think the Revolution was a train wreck. Among the masses, however, Revolution Day is a major holiday.

Other Holidays. There are other non-religious holidays, such as Navy Day, Flag Day, Mothers' Day, New Year's Day, Benito Juárez's birthday, and more. But this is a Catholic country, and Catholic holidays are major events – very major.

Día de la Virgen de Guadalupe (Day of the Virgin of Guadalupe) – December 12. This holiday celebrates the miraculous appearance the brown-skinned Virgin of Guadalupe made to the Aztec peasant, Juan Diego. (Chapter 12). On each December 12, before the Christmas season begins, tens of thousands of the faithful from all over Mexico make the pilgrimage to the Basilica of Guadalupe in Mexico City. Fiestas in honor of her take place throughout the country amidst fireworks and music; altars adorned in flowers and candles brighten modest home fronts and street corners.

Las Posadas. The nine days before Christmas Eve are known as *Las Posadas,* a holiday invented by Saint Ignatius Loyola in the 16th century. He wanted to eliminate the Aztec celebration honoring *Nanahuatl,* the Aztec god who sacrificed himself in fire so that he could be reborn and shine on earth. Saint Ignatius wanted to teach the Indians about Christ instead. So the days the Aztecs devoted to *Nanahuatl* were replaced with nine days of reenacting Mary and Joseph's journey from Nazareth to Bethlehem.

Nochebuena (Christmas Eve) – December 24. On Christmas Eve the faithful flock to Church for the midnight Mass of the Rooster (*Misa de Gallo*). Midnight mass is not always precisely at midnight, but no matter when it actually takes place, at the stroke of midnight church bells fill the air – accompanied by rockets left over from the bombardment of the last local festival. Bells and rockets are today's way of sending the message of Christ's birth. The original message was sent quite differently.

It has been said that a rooster was first to announce the birth of Jesus and that there were a lot of other animals at the scene of the nativity too (even though the Bible says absolutely nothing about animals being there). The presence of animals at the birth of Christ didn't get into Christmas lore until about the time of Saint Francis of Assisi (the Patron Saint of Animals) in the 13th century CE.

According to legend, not only did a rooster announce the birth of Christ, he crowed it in Latin – *"Christus natus est!"* – (Christ is born!). The other animals chimed in as well – also in Latin. (My dogs think that that the whole idea of animals speaking in Latin is *"ridiculum."*)

Following Mass, at least in our neighborhood, partying continues on the streets until dawn. Massive bonfires blaze in the middle of the cobblestone streets. In addition to keeping the party goers warm, the street fires are used to cook *menudo*, a dish widely favored in Mexico. The ingredients consist of beef intestines claimed to have the texture of fine calamari – to *menudos* detractors, it has the texture of a rubber hose. The tripe is boiled in a concoction of lime, chopped onions, cilantro, oregano and crushed red peppers mixed into a red chili base. Some say it gets better after being chilled and reheated. I wouldn't know. While *menudo* is a Christmas dish, it also surfaces regularly Sunday mornings as a cure for hangovers, and for the health- minded, it is high in vitamins A and C.

Día de Los Santos Reyes (Three Kings Day) – January 6. This is the day when Mexicans exchange gifts in keeping with the tradition started by three wise men who brought gifts to baby Jesus. In our modest neighborhood, my wife and I were always amazed at the Christmas presents received by the small children. The children did not seem at all disheartened by the difficulty they were having navigating their roller blades and tricycles over cobblestone streets and broken sidewalks. We had one of the better sidewalks and therefore got to know most of the kids on the block.

Inasmuch as the subject has again turned to our neighborhood, one last comment about that noisy rooster from Bethlehem. In addition to his crowing in Latin, he is said to be the first rooster ever to have crowed before the sun came up. He may have been the first, but the roosters in our neighborhood were determined that he not be the last. Our roosters crowed whenever they felt like it – mostly right outside our bedroom window – or so it seemed.

Día de San Antonio de Abad (Blessing of the Animals) – January 17. On this special day, you can decorate your burro with flowers and ribbons and bring your beast of burden to church to worship with you. This is the Festival of Animals. Cats and dogs are also welcome.

Día de la Candelaria (Day of Candlemas) – February 2. This is the mid-point between the winter solstice and the spring equinox, something like Groundhog Day, and thought to be a predictor of weather. In Mexico the day takes on a religious significance. Baby dolls in the image of Christ are taken to church to be blessed in recognition of Mary taking Jesus to be blessed after his birth – they are then put away until next Christmas.

Semana Santa and Pascua (Holy Week and Easter). In Mexico, where nearly everyone is Catholic, it is no surprise that *Semana Santa* (Easter Week) and *Pascua* (the following week) top the list of all of Mexico's holidays. During this two week period the country's business essentially stops and Mexicans let their hair down after the sacrifices of Lent. Flowered-bedecked altars spring up on the sidewalks in front of village homes. Purple and white pennants, strung from the tops of roofs, crisscross the narrow streets of villages.

On Palm Sunday in Ajijic a bearded young man rides a donkey through town to the decorated courtyard of San Andrés Church. He is wearing a scarlet robe. He heads down a cobblestone street covered with a thick carpet of green palms. He and a parade of men, women, and children in robes and turbans are reenacting the triumphal entry of Jesus to the gates of Jerusalem. Tourists bring up the rear. This is the start of the "Passion Play" which reenacts the last days of the life of Jesus. Village streets are the stage and villagers are the actors.

The pace of Easter activity picks up on Maundy Thursday when the Last Supper is commemorated and the crucifixion of Jesus approaches. On Good Friday, following a lengthy re-enactment of the condemnation of Jesus in the Church yard, Jesus, bleeding from a crown of thorns wedged on his head, is prodded by javelins as he drags the Cross on which he is to be crucified over the cobblestone streets. The Roman guards are in full dress complete with breast plates, red plumed silver helmets, and leg guards up to the hems of their armored skirts. They, together with others in biblical attire, parade beneath floral arches to the Stations of the Cross. The Crucifixion is next to be reenacted. Then, on *Domingo de Gloria*

(Easter Sunday), the faithful pack the church pews to celebrate the hope the Resurrection promises. Such is the Passion Play in our little town, and in countless Mexican villages like it.

And, in Mexico City's crowded borough of Iztapalapa on Good Friday, two million people crowd the streets to witness the same performance.[128] It may be an old play out of an old play book, but it has endured the test of time.

Church-State Relations

*T*he Bible says: *"Render unto Caesar the things that are Caesar's, and render unto God the things that are God's"* (Matthew 22:21). These were the words of Jesus in response to a trick question to trap him into taking a dangerous stand on whether Jews should pay taxes to Rome. That was the question in the days of Jesus. The question today is much the same as it was over 2000 years ago, but it is framed differently: **Should the Church submit to earthly authority?**

To Thomás Garrido Canabal the answer would have been **"ALWAYS."** He was a socialist and atheist whose paramilitary groups, known as *Red Shirts,* sang the socialist anthem while they terrorized Catholics. He was a farmer and on his farm he had a bull named *God,* a cow named *Mary*, and a donkey named *Christ.* He was also the governor of Tabasco, which he tried to make a socialist state. He had a few pet peeves other than with the Catholics: While Governor, he issued decrees against corsets, alcohol, and tombstones.[129] But he went a little too far in 1935 when, as Secretary of Agriculture, he ordered his *Red Shirts* to kill Catholic activists in Mexico City. Canabal was discharged from his government job and exiled to Costa Rica.

Rodrigo Aguilar Alemán would have answered the biblical question just the opposite – he would have replied **"NEVER."** He was a priest hanged from a mango tree in 1927. As the noose was being placed around his neck, he gave his rosary to one of his executioners. When asked **"Who Lives?"** the executioners expected to hear ,**"The Supreme Government."** Instead they heard, **"Christ the King and Blessed Mary of Guadalupe."**

He didn't change the answer despite being bounced up and down on the hangmen's rope three times.[130]

Canabal and Alemán were twentieth century Mexicans with drastically different takes on the question that was posed to Jesus two thousand years earlier. Of course, no one in the New World had reason to debate separation of powers until about 1519. That was the year Cortés landed on Moctezuma's shores. Chances are that any Indian who whispered that the Aztec King should play second fiddle to the supreme deity, Huitzilopochtli, would soon find himself on a one-way hike to the top of the nearest pyramid. So the issue of Church-State relations really never came up until after the Spaniards arrived. Since then, however, Mexico has been immersed in finding the right balance. After nearly five-hundred years of slugging it out it still doesn't seem to have the answer.

Let's take another look at those years – this time in the context the Church played in shaping Mexico's affairs of State.

The Church-State relationship got off to a promising start. A friar named Bartolomé de Olmedo and a priest named Juan Díaz were sent on the high seas along with Cortés to balance the powers between Church and King. Cortés and the clergy were on the same boat, both figuratively and literally. It was not until they got ashore that there were grumblings on the part of the clergy. Friar Bartolomé urged the Conquistadors to stop smashing the Indians idols – he pleaded with the Conquistadors to show the Indians Christian love and the Indians "will destroy their idols by their own decision."[131] This crack in Church-State relations would not be the last. The clergy kept pestering the King about how the Indians were abused. The King warded off his critics by allowing the clergy to monitor the treatment of Indians. It was smooth sailing for awhile, but by 1767 the King had had more than enough. He expelled the Jesuits. Then the seas got choppy. The King set out to reconfigure the role of the Church. Clerical orders were replaced by the "regular" clergy who were responsive to the Crown. Secular universities were founded. The message was clear enough – the King was manning the helm.

But the King was about to be thrown overboard. So when Independence came in 1821 the Church had another chance. Mexico then went on to crown a very conservative Roman Catholic as its Emperor. But Iturbide's reign as Emperor Augustn I only lasted ten months. And just how devout of a Catholic was he? He certainly could not have been the Church's top choice. Some years earlier he had honored one Good Friday by shooting three hundred excommunicated wretches,[132] not exactly the kind of behavior the Pope would have expected from a conservative. The

124

Pope must have wondered what would happen if Mexico ever got a *real* president. He could take comfort in knowing that under the *Plan of Iguala* only Catholics could be Mexican citizens, but most everything else was up for grabs.

Guadalupe Victoria became a *real* president and, lo and behold, under him the Church came out pretty much unscathed. A Constitution was adopted in 1824 that retained the monopoly of the Catholic Church. It was not everything the Church had wanted, but the Pope realized it could have been a whole lot worse. The Church could breath easy – at least for the time being.

The years that followed were chaotic ones. The State was not keeping its eyes on the Church, but even if it had, the State was not strong enough to do anything about the Church. The liberals who instigated Independence kept close eyes on the Church, however – and they didn't like what they were looking at. The wealth and power of the Church was enormous. The Church owned between one-quarter and one-half of Mexico's land.[133] Church buildings were ostentatious and crammed with gold-leafed altars. Figures of Saints, dripping with precious stones, were encased in silver boxes that hung on Church walls. The Church had become a far cry from the simple life it preached to the faithful. A Methodist magazine put it this way:

"To what purpose was this enormous wealth employed? To feed the hungry, clothe the naked, teach the ignorant? Nay, but to consolidate Church authority and extend Church influence, to crush all liberal aspirations and uphold ancient abuses, political as well as ecclesiastical." [134]

Then came Benito Juárez and the anti-church laws he authored. Under the Reform Laws, when the local priest walked into town for groceries he had to dress like everyone else at the market; he was allowed fewer Church holidays and was told how much he could charge the poor for baptisms. Gone were the days when church bells would peel relentlessly. These and the other Reform Laws of the mid-1800s did more than cramp the church – they they hog-tied it.

The Constitution enacted in 1857 added insult to injury. It *denied* the Catholic Church the status of being the "State" religion and went on to adopt much of the liberal agenda. Pope Pius IX lambasted the constitution as *"...corrupting manners...and tearing souls away from our Most Holy Religion...."*[135] It was the end of public morality as far as he was concerned. The Pope also had some harsh words to say about the freedoms of expression the new constitution promised. To the Pope, " [the Constitution] ... *admits the right of pronouncing in public every kind of thought and opinion....* " [136]

Catholics were confused. Did not secular education conflict with the Catholic mission to spread the word of Jesus? The new constitution spoke of freedom from compulsory servitude – did that mean that nuns and priests could forsake their vows?

What had been a bitter confrontation between Church and State quickly turned into a real war. The Reform War went from 1858 to 1861 (Chapter 15). It was during that war when the Church excommunicated people who swore allegiance to the new constitution (as many had to do to get a job). So, did Mexicans then have to choose between being a Catholic or being a traitor? Was that not the question posed to Jesus?

The French invasion (1864) provided new hope for the Church. Napoleon Bonaparte was a believer in God. But Napoleon also voiced many criticisms of organized religion.[137] His choice to preside over Mexico, Maximilian I, disappointed the Church when Maximilian talked of religious freedom and supported a few of the Juárez laws. None of that mattered much anyway because the French were soon ousted. For the Church it was then a matter of waiting it out. Maybe with the French gone, the tide would turn. But if the Church thought that a new constitution would shine light in its favor, it was in for another disappointment. The Constitution of 1917 (which is the current Constitution) institutionalized many "anti- Church" reforms. And, lest the Church have any doubts, the Constitution added this for good measure:

"Neither in public nor in private... [shall the Church] ...ever have the right to criticize the basic laws of the Country... the authorities...the government in general; ...nor the right to associate for political purposes."

That didn't stop the Archbishop of Mexico from complaining. He announced to the press that Roman Catholics could no longer in good conscience accept the Mexican Constitution. Then President Calles, who was never known to be bashful, came out swinging. He disbanded religious processions, deported foreign priests and nuns, closed church schools and shut down monasteries and convents.

The Archbishop responded by having the clergy go on strike. That meant no masses, baptisms, or last rites. The Church also attempted an economic boycott. But "peaceful" measures were just the beginning. The salvos turned to war. It was the Cristeros versus Calles. The Cristero War began in 1926. Three years and 90,000 lives later it was over. (Chapter 16). It ended by a truce brokered by the United States, but the killings continued.

The war was still smoldering when president-elect Álvaro Obregón attended a banquet in his honor. An artist by the name of Toral was painting scenes of the banquet, but Toral had in mind something other than painting portraits of the dignitaries eating. Toral was a religious fanatic who was "fighting" the war against the State, but in somewhat of a non-conventional manner. In among his art supplies, he had a pistol from which he unloaded five shots into the president-elect's head. Toral's trial re-stirred the Church-State frenzy. Toral was found guilty and received the death sentence.

Bickering between Church and State went on and on. In 1934 Cárdenas was elected President and he orchestrated something of a détente. The next president, Álvila Comacho (1940-1946) tried repealing some anti-church laws but most remained intact. Catholic schools were allowed to open under Comacho but only under the guise of private institutions.

In the early 1980's the Church accused Mexico of being a democracy in "theory" only. A few years later bishops in Juárez and Chihuahua denounced electoral fraud. Did not such claims violate the Constitution's ban on Church criticism of government? The State thought it did and volleyed with a few barbs of its own. Then the Church responded again, this time with a mixed message – it being that, while priests should be above politics, they have a moral duty to denounce actions that violate Christian morality.

In 1992 President Salinas set out to establish a better relationship between Church and State by allowing churches to own their buildings and allowing preachers to vote. But it was also under Salinas's presidency that the Chiapas rebellion occurred (Chapter 13) during which local Church officials backed the rebels. In May of 2000, just following a bishops' conference in Mexico City, the bishops warned the people of Mexico about electoral fraud and proclaimed that failure to vote in the upcoming presidential election would be a "moral sin." The Minister of the Interior took this as a direct slam against the PRI, then Mexico's ruling party. The Minister shot back that the Church was not to meddle in State affairs.

In March of 2012 Pope Benedict XVI visited Mexico and met with then President Caulderón. There was speculation that one purpose of the visit was to rally support for constitutional changes that would weaken secular institutions, guarantee religious education in public schools, allow the Church freedom to own and operate mass print and electronic mass media, and intervene in politics.[138]

As of the time of this writing, Peña Nieto is the President of Mexico. He was a governor in 2010 when he and his girlfriend visited the Pope on a tour to promote the art of his state. Nieto caused eyebrows to rise when he announced his wedding plans to the Pope before telling his fellow countrymen.[139] Perhaps Nieto, then an aspiring politician, was signaling a new era of openness in Church-State relations. Time will tell.

The State cannot change the fact that just about all Mexicans are Catholic. Mexico is a very Catholic country. The presence of the Church is everywhere despite a national framework of laws and institutions that are decidedly secular. But, Mexico's anti-church laws have a long history of being enforced at the whim of the president. While the laws have been softened from time to time, the State makes strong efforts to keep displays of faith under the church belfry and to keep the Church out of politics.

Despite all the back and forth between Church and State, and perhaps because of it, the Church continues to be firmly implanted in the hearts and souls of Mexico's people. Still, the Church remains challenged to render unto Caesar the things that are best left in the hands of Caesar. Perhaps the real issue is defining what those "things" are. Mexico has the second biggest Catholic population in the world (behind Brazil);[140] most of Mexico's people are poor; and, among the poor, many families are too big. Yet the Church continues to ban contraception. Which side is right? The Catholic Church has condemned Mexico City's legalization of same-sex marriages and relaxation of its abortion laws despite a rising tide in favor of both. What should be the role of the Church in these matters? The Bishop of Querétero published a website text on "the evils of feminism."[141] Is this what bishops are supposed to be doing in their spare time? If the Church's position on stem cell research and euthanasia are non-negotiable, should the State take action anyway? These are just a few of the issues of today. Tomorrow there will be others.

Intellectuals can debate the biblical question and whether the spiritual world transcends the earthly affairs of State. The Roman soldiers were not able to ambush the Prince of Peace two thousand years ago because Jesus dodged the question. Perhaps he had a message for today. As long as there are both worlds, folks on the street know that the State must keep a watchful eye on the Church – and, vice versa.

Food, Markets & Music

The Norwegians have *lefse*; the Scottish have *bannock*; the Irish have *potato farls;* Italians have *pizza*; the Indians have *naan*; the English have *muffins;*Armenians have *lavash*. Just about every country has a traditional unleavened bread. In Mexico, it is the *tortilla*.

One could not imagine that a lefse shortage could topple King Harold V of Norway nor that the Brits would ever storm Buckingham Palace over the price of muffins, but, in Mexico, it somehow seems imaginable that overpriced tortillas could spark a revolution. In January, 2007, tens of thousands of Mexicans marched through Mexico City protesting a 400% price increase in the price of *tortillas*.[142] That was a devastating increase to poor people who were already spending a third of their wages on tortillas.

The natives had been eating *tortillas* for a very long time; in fact, they sold them to the Conquistadors. They developed cultivated corn 10,000 years ago. They figured out how to mill the strange yellow kernels into dough called *masa* and hand shape and fry the *masa* to make tortillas. Some Mexicans still hand slap the *masa* into the shape of the *tortilla*; some use small wood or metal presses, but the old methods are giving way to *tortilla* factories scattered on side streets throughout Mexico. These mostly small family operations have machines that stamp out the *masa* into *tortillas* and lower them on to an assembly line where they are lightly fried, then they are weighed and hand-packaged. Mothers and children buy a warm stack early in the day and the *tortillas* become the core ingredient of the meals to follow that day. These are corn *tortillas,* much preferred by Mexicans – corn *tortillas* are not to be confused with the longer shelf-life and less nutritional wheat *tortillas*.

While Mexico is well known for *tortillas,* what may be less known is that it is the birthplace of chocolate. Chocolate is made from the beans of the cocoa tree. Moctezuma had a "divine" beverage called *chocolatl,* a concoction of chocolate, vanilla and spices. It was served cold, the consistency of maple syrup, and was said to permit a man to walk a whole day without food. Moctezuma served it in a golden goblet to Cortés. Cortés loved it. The Conquistadors took cocoa plants back to Spain and before long chocolate drinks became the rage throughout Europe. Centuries later it was made into solid chocolates we know today.

The food of Mexico today is largely the result of the Conquistadors introducing European food culture into the food culture of the native Indians, and vice versa. But it is fanciful to suggest the blending of the food cultures was driven by anything other than necessity. The Aztecs wanted no part of the Conquistadors, say nothing of sharing recipes with them. When Moctezuma was told that Cortés had landed on Moctezuma's shores, Moctezuma sent emissaries to the coast bearing gifts to Cortés hoping the Conquistadors would go back home – wherever that was. The bribes did not work. They just egged the Conquistadors on. The Conquistadors then showed up at Moctezuma's draw bridge. Moctezuma knew he had better make the Conquistadors happy, so he hosted a royal feast, hoping that would satisfy them. The Conquistadors were not to be bought off that easily. They were hungry, but their hunger was for silver and gold.

While the Conquistadors never found all the gold and silver they hoped for, they discovered a treasure trove of new foods – new to them, that is. In addition to corn and chocolate, the Indians taught the Conquistadors about beans, squash, tomatoes, avocados, chilies, coconuts, peanuts, and pulque (Mexico's traditional alcoholic beverage made from the sap of the sacred maguey plant). The Conquistadors returned the favor. They taught the natives about pork, beef, lamb, cheese, milk, vinegar, olive oil, cinnamon, coriander, oregano, black pepper, apples, oranges, grapes, and, of course, wine. But it was not a complete blending of food cultures. The Indians could not tempt the Conquistadors with native delicacies, like snakes, monkeys, grasshoppers, caterpillars, locusts, and ant eggs.

When the French occupied Mexico for a short period in the 19th century they brought with them a variety of baked goods such as sweet breads (*pan dulce*) and hard rolls (*bolillos).* Add to the mix the flavors of Europe's other countries, Africa, Asia, and the Caribbean, and the end result is some of the best food in the world – The Mexican Cuisine.

Much of Mexico's great food can be purchased on the streets, including in my neighborhood where families cater to their friends and neighbors on white plastic furniture emblazed with Coke and Corona logos. Street food is just a small part of Mexico's huge informal economy where knock-off

Rolex watches are hawked to skeptical tourists; where look-alike Calvin Kline blue jeans are piled high on make-shift counters set on vacated streets; where bracelets, earrings, and blankets are sold in the park. (For a shopper with a good eye for value, they often are hand-made and of exceptional quality.) In this informal economy there is no state mechanism to keep track of sales (nor to tax them); nor is much government money spent on sanitation or working conditions. Almost 30% of Mexican workers scrounge out a living in this world.[143] It is a world of no benefits, cash registers, credit cards – and little accountability. Nevertheless, in my neighborhood it appeared that the system worked well and that it provided a much needed social safety net. Perhaps most important, it gives people work, engenders pride and self-respect, and solidifies a strong sense of community. Perhaps that is what keeps the country going.

© Enrique Velázquez / Lic.courtesy of Belva y Enrique Velázquez Studio, Ajijic • www.mymexicoart.com

The quaint scene above is a far cry from Guadalajara's bustling *Libertad Mercado*. There, in the narrow aisles of this gigantic three story downtown complex, are some 2600-3000 vendors jammed into stalls brimming with foods and goods of every description: racks of pig heads, plucked chickens dangling upside down by their feet, slabs of raw meats harpooned on overhead steel hooks, fish on melting ice, vegetables and fruits piled high, crates of spices and herbs, song birds in wicker cages, lavish displays of flowers, Mexican candies, TV sets, calculators, radios, kitchen blenders, sombreros, leather boots, shoes, belts, sportswear, jewelry, and – you name it. I could go on, but you got the point.

Folks in the U.S. who are used to shopping at Whole Foods or Nordstrom's may find *Libertad Mercado* something of a culture shock – but they should go anyway. This is a place worthy of its popular name, *San Juan de Dios* (named after a nearby church). Well, maybe the reference to "God" is a bit of a stretch – but thousands of people make a shopping pilgrimage there every day. It is a Moroccan bazaar without the cobras – a power shopper's dream come true.

Despite the invasion of the big box stores, shopping malls, supermarkets, department stores and home building centers, the *Mercado* (covered market) and the *tianguis* (open air market) continue their hold upon Mexicans of all economic strata. In today's food craze the bountiful displays and unending selections of fresh foods (and the absence of processed foods) reinforces the hope that these institutions will last forever.

Unless you are totally deaf, you cannot be anywhere near Guadalajara's *Mercado Libertad* without being swept next door and into the *Plaza de los Mariachis* (Plaza of the Mariachis). There, these masters of the guitar, trumpet and violin– in bold-colored charro outfits studded in shining metal

– get better with every beer. Through the fog of beer and a shot or two of tequila these mariachis with their powerful voices are a match for the world famous Three Tenors.

Actually, one of the Three Tenors, Plácido Domingo, in his early years, performed in Guadalajara's stately opera house, *Teatro Degollado,* just a few blocks (within 'earshot,' so to speak) of the *Plaza de los Mariachis.* In 1959, he played the role of Pascual in the opera *Marina* – and then performed as Borsa in *Rigoletto.*[144] Plácido Domingo, of course, was not destined to sing in mariachi bands. Still, it is noteworthy that many of his early years were spent in Mexico. Here it must be hastily pointed out that mariachi music is not to be confused with opera. But mariachi music, one might argue, can be every bit as powerful, melodious, and enchanting as an operatic aria.

Nor should mariachi music be confused with Gregorian chants. Pope Gregory would not have confused the two (even though he is credited with inventing the chants) because mariachi music was unheard of in the 7th century. But some 1000 years later in Mexico – 1852, to be more precise – Father Cosme Santa Anna made the distinction, and he made it with a vengeance. That was the year he wrote a letter to his bishop complaining about the noisy band playing across from his church in Rosamorado, Nayarit,[145] a city not too far from Guadalajara.   He ordered the band to stop the irreverent music and, to make sure they did stop, he hijacked their instruments. His priestly garb must have done the trick because the rest of that evening was quiet and peaceful in Rosamorado.

Aside from this extraordinary act of bravery, his letter to the bishop is significant because, before then, no one had figured out where the word *mariachi* came from. It used to be thought that the word was a corruption of the French word for *marriage* and that it came into use in Mexico during the brief reign of Emperor Maximilian (1864-1867). History buffs can thank Father Cosme for setting the historical record straight. His letter complaining to the bishop contains the word *mariachi* marking its first appearance (in print) on record. The letter was dated more than a decade before France ever thought of invading Mexico. So much for the French connection.

Let's just say that nobody knows where the word came from, and probably few people care. What people do care about is the music. In November of 2011, UNESCO put mariachi music on its list of important cultural traditions.[146] Today there are mariachi schools, mariachi classes, and mariachi degrees in many countries, including the United States, Japan, and Columbia.[147] With that kind of following, it's hard to understand what the pious Padre Cosme was complaining about. Maybe he was just a grouch.

Mariachi music is string, brass, and powerful voices. The lyrics tell of lost loves, rebellions, death, and national pride. The classic, at least here in Guadalajara, is the city's anthem by that name. The expressions on the musicians' faces tell more than the lyrics.

There is not much to suggest that mariachi music had roots tied to Indian music. Indian music was rhythmic, repetitious, and had a tight melodic range. The Indians made their music from drums, gourds, turtle shells, and flutes. It would go on for hours as part of a religious ritual or to honor a nobleman. The rhythm section tried very hard not to miss a beat as doing so could offend the gods, for which the punishment was death.

The Spanish newcomers didn't like Indian music. They were

accustomed to solemn church music, elegies to mourn deaths, and celebratory music to inspire the King's subjects. There was another reason the Colonists didn't like Indian music. They didn't like the sensual movements of natives who danced to it. The Colonists' biggest problem with Indian music, however, was the fear that Indian music would return the Indians to their pagan gods. So they outlawed it.

Nevertheless, the clergy recognized that the Indians loved music. The clergy soon came to the realization that the singing of mass could attract the Indians to Christianity. The first bishop of Mexico, Juan de Zumárraga, believed that Indians were converted to Christianity more by music than by anything else.[148]

People who may be offended by bawdy mariachi music – like Father Cosme was – and people who may be horrified by lewd body movements made to the clinking of turtle shells – like the friars were – can take comfort in knowing that Mexico has many other genres of song and dance. A good sampling of the folk tradition can be experienced at performances of the internationally acclaimed *Ballet Folklórico* in cities large and small throughout Mexico and most of the world.

© Belva Velázquez / Lic.courtesy of Belva y Enrique Velázquez Studio, Ajijic • www.mymexicoart.com

Author's note. This chapter could lead the reader to the false conclusion that folk music is the only music of Mexico when, in fact, it is just a small, but colorful, part of it. Bigger cities have elegant opera houses, and smaller cities have attractive and well-attended venues, all of which host symphonies and operas from the cultural capitols of the world, including those in Mexico. And every kind of music, from hip-hop to jazz, is listened to and danced to in Mexico's night clubs and discotheques.

Wealth

$\mathcal{T}$*he Distribution of Wealth in Mexico*[149] is a relatively obscure essay published in 1940. Its author, Federico Bach, was a Mexican economist and lecturer. He has been described as a known Marxist who at one time was expelled from Mexico as a "Communist agitator."[150] That may be, but his piece on Mexico's wealth is worth reading.

Bach writes that Mexico's natural "wealth" was exaggerated from the start. The Cortés expedition was essentially a "for profit" venture financed in large part by investors whom Cortés needed to keep in an optimistic frame of mind by overstating the riches to be gained; the wealth of the mines and farms could only have been profitably extracted if the hard work was done on the backs of virtually enslaved poor people. Bach argues that Mexico was never very rich to begin with, that the wealth that did exist was distributed wrongly, and that any hope for Mexico depended on realignment of its wealth.

Bach's writings were before *maquiladoras"* were ever heard of; before the plight of the small farmer was made worse by NAFTA; before a new crop of billionaires was created by privatizing telecommunications and banks: before the mismanagement of Mexico's oil resources; before drug trafficking created yet a new class of the very rich.

Today about 10% of Mexicans are regarded as being rich.[151] Of the Forbes list of the world's 1500 individuals with a net worth of one billion dollars or more, eleven are Mexicans. And, according to Forbes, Mexico's Carlos Slim Helu is the world's richest man.[152] (But don't hold his money against him; he is a greatly admired philanthropist who is said to live modestly; shuns yachts and private jet planes, and drives himself to work.)

The middle class accounts for approximately 30% of the population.[153]

That leaves more than one-half as being poor. But "poor" and "poverty stricken" are different things. For those who need statistics to prove what is in plain sight, there are other numbers: over one-half of Mexicans live on less than $2 a day ("poverty"),[154] and about one-half of those live on less than $1 a day ("extreme poverty").[155] The ranks of Mexico's poor extend from the indigenous rural peoples in the south, where children wash windshields for a peso before the light turns green, to the assembly plant *maquiladora* workers in the north whose pathetic circumstances have already been described.

Let's look at it another way. Again according to Forbes, the average earnings of Mexican workers is 230 pesos a day or $6,600 (U.S.) per year.[156] Here, of course, we are talking about people who work in a country that is generally perceived to have a relatively low cost of living. Still, not many working Mexicans earning $6600 a year would consider themselves to be financially secure, say nothing of feeling "well-off."

About the time Bach was publishing *The Distribution of Wealth in Mexico,* a person of international renown, who was very much absorbed in the subject of wealth distribution, got axed in the head while living in Mexico. His name was Leon Trotsky, a Communist leader and writer who had been instrumental in the 1917 Russian Revolution, but who was detested by his boss, Joseph Stalin. The feeling between them was mutual. Trotsky was expelled from the Soviet Union in 1929. He tried living in Turkey, then in France, and then in Norway, but Stalin kept the pressure on those countries to oust Trotsky. Trotsky did not appear to be welcome anywhere until Diego Rivera, the noted Mexican muralist, came to his rescue.

When Diego Rivera was not painting murals portraying the plight of the poor and disadvantaged, he was out mingling with Communists. One of his murals, *Man at the Crossroads,* was commissioned by Nelson Rockefeller for the ground floor of New York City's Rockefeller Center. Diego seized an opportunity to use the Rockefeller fortunes to impart a message dear to Diego's heart: he painted the face of Lenin on a part of the mural. Mr. Rockefeller was not amused, but that is another story.

Trotsky and Rivera were friends; as were Rivera and Mexico's President Lázaro Cárdenas. You have read that Cárdenas was a champion of the poor. He aggressively redistributed land (*ejidos*), advanced education, reformed labor unions, and you will read that he nationalized the nation's oil. He flirted with Communism and surrounded himself with Stalinists. Trotsky described Cárdenas as the greatest leader of the world but mused that he was not far enough to the left.

Rivera persuaded President Cárdenas to allow Trotsky and his wife, Natalia, to live in Mexico. So Trotsky slipped out of Norway on a freighter headed for Tampico, Mexico. There, Trotsky and his wife were transported by a special train to take them to Mexico City where the Trotskys moved in with Diego Rivera and his wife, Frida Kahlo.

Frida Kahlo was a renowned artist in her own right. She, like her husband, was active in Communist circles. Her family home (and the home in which she and Diego from time to time lived, and the home in which Frida died) was called *Casa Azul* (Blue House). It was (and still is) located in a fashionable tree-shaded neighborhood of Mexico City known as Coyoacán.

The Trotskys settled into Frida's *Casa Azul*. The marriage between Frida and Diego was a turmultous one. Trotsky, whom Frida called the "old man," had an affair with Frida. But this story is not about Frida's trysts– even though there is said to be more to write about.

Trotsky became integrated into socialistic causes in Mexico. He was a prolific writer and was extremely critical of Stalin – a dangerous stand to take despite the ocean between them. Trotsky feared for his life. The Blue House started to resemble a fort. Books were loaded on window sills to absorb gunfire. Diego bought the house next door for additional protection. The Trotskys then moved to a more secure and heavily guarded home in Coyoacán. The better security didn't pay off. On August 20, 1940, an undercover agent for Stalin managed to gain entry into Trotsky's study where he delivered a fatal blow to Trotsky with an ice axe. The blow was poorly delivered and Trotsky managed to live long enough to say: "Stalin has finally accomplished the task he attempted unsuccessfully before."[157]

Today, if you were looking to buy a really nice house in Coyoacán you better have a hefty bank account and plan to employ household staff so as not to be frowned upon by your neighbors. Back in the days of the Trotskys, Frida, and Diego, the neighborhood was upscale too. Given their political inclinations, this seems like an unlikely neighborhood for them to have hung out, but the two internationally-renowned artists and the internationally-renowned exile and his wife would not be expected to live in poverty. Diego and Frida called Coyoacán "home" and Trotsky had little choice in the matter. Their true soul brothers, however, were living on another side of town, in Netzahual-coyotl, Mexico's fourth largest city. There, some one million of Mexico's very poor struggled to exist, many in one room shanties built on the muddy floor of what had been Moctezuma's Lake Texcoco.

Federico Bach, Leon and Natalia Trotsky, Diego Rivera, and Frida

Kahlo could hardly be described as "peas in the same pod," but they all shared some common notions of economic and social justice which they expressed in very different ways. No doubt, if they were living today, there would be more essays to write and more murals to paint.

Oil

$\mathcal{S}$ ome years before Cortés, black gunk oozed up from the ground, but the ancient Olmec natives didn't know what it was nor what to do with it; that is, until one of them figured out that it was just the thing for waterproofing canoes. By the turn of the twentieth century, the world was not thinking about canoes, however. The industrialized nations of the world were thinking about battleships. And, foreign entrepreneurs were quick to grasp that oil was then to Mexico what silver had been when Mexico was a colony of Spain.

A British/Dutch company and an American company got their rigs pumping in Mexico by the early 1900s. They not only got the jump on other foreign investors, they beat Mexicans to it – and they expected labor in this backward country to be cheap. After all, exploitation of the Mexican worker was nothing new; the Colonists sent the Indians into the silver mines and workers on haciendas were virtual slaves. So what was so special about the Confederation of Mexican Petroleum Workers? The Union went on strike. An arbitration panel debunked the "inability to pay" defense raised by the oil companies. The oil companies threatened to pull stakes. Mexico's President Cárdenas decided to sit down at the bargaining table. He promised that the Union would call off the strike if the oil companies paid what the arbitration panel figured was rightfully owed to the workers. Talks with the President got downright nasty. The oil captains said the President couldn't call off the strike even if he wanted to. That was the wrong thing to say. Instead of calling off the strike, Cárdenas called off the meeting and nationalized the companies' oil and the foreigners' rigs, thus giving birth to PEMEX, Mexico's state- controlled oil monopoly. The Mexicans were jubilant. Thousands cheered in the streets of Mexico City. Wealthy women were so proud of their country for kicking the foreigners out they donated jewelry to help pay the expropriation costs.

The celebrating did not last long, however. On the heels of nationalizing the nation's oil, the United States, Britain, and Holland retaliated by boycotting Mexican oil. That was the foreigners' second mistake. The boycott didn't look like such a good idea by the time World War II came on and Mexico was poised to sell oil to Hitler. The boycott was dropped.

The ups and downs of PEMEX could fill chapters. Despite vast reserves and being one of the world's largest oil producers, Mexico's oil production is on the decline, some say, due to underinvestment in exploration and production. The concern is that, as domestic demand increases, Mexico is trending toward becoming a net importer of oil. Declining production is a problem for Mexico because much of the cost of running Mexico's government depends on oil. Oil has to bear this Herculean burden because street vendors, merchants in food stalls, ladies selling remade used clothes, mariachi bands and the rest of Mexico's so called "informal economy" do not pay taxes – and nobody has figured out how to tax the untold sums of cash that pass "underground" in drug deals. All of these untaxed transactions means that PEMEX must come up with some 40% of the cost of running the country.[158]

Critics of PEMEX blame falling production on bloated bureaucracies, stolen oil, bribes, and inept management. Some favor privatization.

Others blame resistance to foreign investment. But why allow foreign intervention? Did Mexico not learn anything when Spain looted its silver? Did not Mexico learn from the long reign of *The Strong Man,* Porfirio Díaz, that making grand deals with foreign bankers can lead to revolution? Did Mexico forget that the people filled the streets in jubilation when President Cárdenas in 1938 kicked the foreign oil tycoons *out* of Mexico? Mexicans are proud people. Maybe they should stick with keeping their own canoe afloat. Many Mexicans think so.

Border Policy

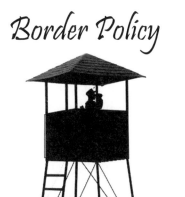

*B*y the time this book goes to print, the movie *Machete* will have come and gone from the theatre near you.

This "R" rated flick has a complicated plot. The action is over the top. One of the movie's many story lines involves its hero, a Rambo-like Mexican named Machete, who works as a gardener in the U.S. illegally (without "documents"). He is hired to assassinate a Texas senator running for reelection on an immigration platform that compares undocumented Mexicans to leeches. Sorry, you will have to rent the movie if you care how it comes out. But those who can sit through all the sex and violence will get the message of Hollywood's rejection of the anti-immigrant crowd.

Few issues have riled the public more than that of illegal immigration, particularly when the immigrants cross over from Mexico. Voices of moderation are drowned out by extremes. Take this quotation:

"The situation is simple. A hostile foreign power is using its criminal underclass to colonize the United States. The federal government, having been hijacked by the radical left, is doing everything it can to assist this invasion, in the belief that creating a massive new underclass and reducing Caucasians to minority status will give them the demographic leverage to impose socialism and one party rule." [159]

There's more: Another source reports that anti-immigration activists have launched *"a campaign to recruit environmentalists to their cause by blaming immigrants for urban sprawl, over-consumption, and a host of other environmental problems."* [160]

Toxic views are one thing. Camouflaged snipers *"...sitting like hunters waiting for these people to come across,"* [161] or those who would *"line the border with minefields"* [162] are frightfully different.

As this book goes to publication in the spring of 2013, the U.S. Congress is struggling with immigration reform. No matter what may come out of Congress, good border policy is not likely to be discovered on the outer fringes, nor in the movie *Machete.* And, no matter what the law is or what it may become, *attitudes* can linger for decades – they have a way of lagging behind laws (take abortion, race discrimination, feminism, and on-and-on).

So, look at some facts that may, over time, moderate some attitudes.

Illegal immigration is often explained in "push-pull" terms, namely: Mexicans come to the U.S. because there are not enough jobs in Mexico (the "push"), and, Mexicans working in the U.S. earn many times more than what they could earn in Mexico (the "pull"). But wait. If the push-pull factor is the cause, maybe border hysteria will just run out of steam. According to the Mexican Migration Project at Princeton University, since the 2008-2009 financial meltdown the population of undocumented workers in the U.S. actually fell and Mexicans without documents did not migrate at a pace to replace the loss, thus creating a net zero balance for the first time in 50 years. [163] These findings should come as no surprise. Why should young Mexican fathers risk their lives on dangerous night-time treks over deserts and mountains if there is no work at the end of the trail? Why ride the roofs of freight cars if there are no jobs at the end of the line? Why be subjected to state laws that give the police power to detain people *suspected* of being in the U.S. illegally and make it a crime *not* to carry immigration papers? Who wants to be subjected to racial profiling and the humiliation of city rental laws that make housing unavailable? Why go through all of this? Such questions are being asked south of the border.

And some vexing questions are being asked north of the border too. Will a "net zero' migration pattern drain the U.S. of an essential labor pool? The question is asked in an article appearing in the Christian Science Monitor: What will happen if the workers that farmers, hotels, and restaurants have relied on for decades don't come back? Will this have a ripple effect on the rest of the U.S. economy? [164] Law makers are in a pickle. They are keenly aware of the importance of the Hispanic vote. Yet politicians are faced with significant pockets of anti-Mexico sentiment, members of which will have no part of a "path to citizenship" for the 11 million or so undocumented workers in the United States. If that isn't perplexing enough, law makers understand that the Mexicans who cross the border in the black of night contribute massive amounts each year to Social Security;[165] they know that these same people will never collect a dime of Social Security benefits unless they become citizens. They also know that many Mexicans have become deeply rooted in the U.S. with families, friends, and community connections; that the Mexican worker will take jobs others are unwilling to take; that low-paying jobs performed by Mexicans have helped reduce the rate of inflation and helped to make the U.S. more competitive in the world economy.

Law makers are not the only ones in a quandary. The public is too. Many of the "faithful" are taking a second look at Deuteronomy 10:19, Luke 10:27, Romans 13:10, 3 John 1-5, and the many other biblical messages about "welcoming the stranger."

What a conundrum!

Epilogue

I often wonder what might have happened had my banker said no to our Mexico house. I suspect I would have returned to the day-to-day frustrations and occasional rewards that are a part of small town law practice. But I would not have befriended kind and hardworking tradesmen like Armando and Rosendo; it would be unlikely that Lorenzo would have bought his cow – so his neighbors would have had to buy milk elsewhere; Frida, our Mexican dog, would still be in Mexico, probably tethered on a roof; the kitten under the vendor cart would now be a full grown cat, never having been traumatized by our border collie; our Newfoundland, Cricket, would have gone through life never having chased cows down the Lake Chapala shore: Daffy, our basset hound, would have spent her final days under the snowy winter skies of Wisconsin instead of under the bright Mexican sun; several Mexican traffic cops would be a little bit poorer; and, I would never have driven through Possum Grape, nor would I have even heard of the Toad Suck Festival.

But this book is not about me – it is about Mexico and that nation's journey over a rough and rambling road. Wouldn't it be nice if the road ahead looked like this?

Maybe it will.

End Notes

CHAPTER 1

(1) (State Dept. Website) U.S. Department of State, *Mexico,* http://travel.state. gov/travel/cis_pa_tw/cis/cis_970.html (Accessed 6/1/2012).
(2) (Hit by lightning) Mexico Mike, *Safety in Mexico,* http://www.mexicomike. com/safety/safety-UsStateDepartment.html (Accessed: 6/7/2012).

CHAPTER 2

(3) (Busiest Border) Corporation Service Company (CSC), *Biometeric Border Crossing Cards Increase Security Along the World's Busiest Border,* http://www. csc.com/public_sector/case_studies/9220-biometric_border_crossing_cards_ increase_security_along_the_world%E2%80%99s_busiest_border (Accessed: 5/31/2012).
(4) (40+ crossings) U.S. Customs and Border Protection ,*Border Wait Times,* http://apps.cbp.gov/bwt/ (Accessed: 5/31/2012).
(5) (Every 15 seconds) NPR Online, John Burnett, *Drugs Cross Border by Truck, Free Trade and Chance,* http://www.npr.org/templates/story/story. php?storyId=131106638 (Accessed 5/31/2012).
(6) (25-40 billion) James Lange, *From Spas to Banks, Mexico's Economy Rides on Drugs,* Reuters, January 22, 2010, http://www.reuters.com/ article/2010/01/22/us-drugs-mexico-economy-idUSTRE60L0X120100122 (Accessed 5/31/2012).
(7) (Most smuggling by truck) U.S. Department of Justice, National Drug Intelligence Center, National Drug Threat Assessment 2010, February, 2010 *Drugs Movement Into and Within the United States,* http://www.justice.gov/ ndic/pubs38/38661/movement.htm (Accessed 5/31/2012).
(8) (1 in 5 inspected)) NPR, John Burnett, *Drugs Cross Border by Truck, Free Trade and Chance,* http://www.npr.org/templates/story/story. php?storyId=131106638 (Accessed 5/31/2012).
(9) (Dodge Dakota) CBS Local 2, Palm Spring CA, http://www.kpsplocal2. com/Content/Headlines/story/Cocaine-Valued-at-1-1-Million-Hidden-in-Trucks/ nGuTV9Of40iL2LeHylx-5A.cspx (Accessed 2011).
(10) (One Ton Marijuana)The Laredo Sun, August 4, 2011, *Truck Driver Arrested on Drug Charges,* http://www.laredosun.us/notas.asp?id=17677 (Accessed 5/31/2012).
(11) (Tunnel)" Jessica Hopper, "Smugglers Use Catapult to Launch Bales of Pot Across Border," January 27, 2011, *World News with Diane Sawyer,* ABC News, http://abcnews.go.com/US/drug-smugglers-catapult-launch-marijuana-arizona-mexico-border/story?id=12776586 (Accessed 5/31/2012).
(12) (100 tunnels) Patrick Radden Keefe , "The Snow Kings of Mexico," *New York Times Magazine,* Sunday Edition, June 23, 2012 , 43.

(13) (Raft) MAXIMUMNEWSINFORMER.COM *Texas Choppers Pilots Chase Smugglers Over Rio Grande* http://maximumnewsinformer. com/?p=4219 (Accessed 5/31/2012).

(14) (Submersibles) U.S. Department of Justice, National Drug Intelligence Center, National Drug Threat Assessment 2010, February, 2010, *Drugs Movement Into and Within the United States* http://www.justice.gov/ndic/ pubs38/38661/movement.htm (Accessed 5/31/2012)

(15) (Containers) U.S. Department of Justice, National Drug Intelligence Center, National Drug Threat Assessment 2010, *Drugs Movement Into and Within the United States,* , February, 2010, http://www.justice.gov/ndic/ pubs38/38661/movement.htm (Accessed 5/31/2012).

(16) (Airplanes) Daniel Hopsicker, "CIA Drug Planes: 'Tip of the Iceberg' Fleet of 50 American Planes Sold to Mex Cartel," *Mad Cow Morning News*, January 16, 2008   http://www.madcowprod.com/01162008.html (Accessed 5/31/2012)

(17) (Ultralights) Robert Tilford," Mexican Drug Smugglers using ultra-lights to smuggle drugs into US,"*Chatlotte City Buzz Examiner,* January 26, 2012, http://www.examiner.com/article/mexican-drug-smugglers-using-ultralights-to- smuggle-drugs-into-the-us (Accessed 6/28/2012).

(18) (Cataplulter) Jessica Hopper, "Smugglers Use Catapult to Launch Bales of Pot Across Border," January 27, 2011, *World News with Diane Sawyer*, ABC News, http://abcnews.go.com/US/drug-smugglers-catapult-launch-marijuana- arizona-mexico-border/story?id=12776586 (Accessed 5/31/2012).

(19) (Package in Blueberries) John Burnett, "Drugs Cross Border by Truck, Free Trade and Chance," *NPR* http://www.npr.org/templates/story/story. php?storyId=131106638 (Accessed 5/31/2012).

(20) (Addiction-Civil War Disease) Schaffer Library of Drug Policy, Marijuana Business News. Com, Carl Olsen's Marijuana Archive, *The Situation in 1900,* http://www.druglibrary.org/olsen/dpf/whitebread02.html (Accessed 6/27/2012

(21) (Bayer Aspirin) Free Enterprise Land, *A Brand Name Gone Wrong,* http://www.freeenterpriseland.com/BOOK/GONEWRONG.html (Accessed 5/31/2012).

(22) (Sears) Ben Sullivan, *Sears & Roebuck Once Sold Opium, Heroine, and Cocaine,* FOURWINDS10.COM,http://www.fourwinds10.net/siterun_data/ health/drugs/news.php?q=1279171613 (Accessed 5/31/2012),

(23) (Estimated 250,000 Drug Addicts) "http://www.factmonster.com/ce6/sci/ A0857830.html *The Columbia Electronic Encyclopedia.*
© 1994, 2000-2006, on Fact Monster.
© 2000–2007 Pearson Education, publishing as Fact Monster.
28 Jun. 2012 <http://www.factmonster.com/ce6/sci/A0857830.html>. (Accessed 6/27/2012).

(24) (Drugs for Women) Schaffer Library of Drug Policy, Marijuana Business News. Com, Carl Olsen's Marijuana Archive, *The Situation in 1900,* Accessed: 5/31/2012 http://www.druglibrary.org/olsen/dpf/whitebread02.html

(25) (Negro Addiction) Joseph Mcciver M.D. and George K. Price M.D., "Drug Addiction-Analysis of One Hundred and Forty-Seven Cases at the Philadelphia General Hospital," *The Journal of the American Medical Association,* Volume 66, 476-480 http://books.google.com/books?id=yvUbAQ AAMAAJ&pg=PA477&lpg=PA477&dq=journal+american+medical+association+ negroes+drug+sniffing&source=bl&ots=98Rm-J8xkX&sig=y2zhFLAD-ecGmXd_ CsXMgo-IV3Q&hl=en&ei=CJS9ToPTFLT9sQKyv_3pAQ&sa=X&oi=book_result& ct=result&resnum=1&ved=0CB4Q6AEwAA#v=onepage&q&f=false (Accessed 6/1/2012).

(26) (Drugs and Rape) Schaffer Library of Drug Policy, *The Racial Roots of our Drug Laws,* Cites Dr. Chrisopher Koch, Literary Digest, March 28, 1914, 687, http://www.druglibrary.org/schaffer/library/histdrug.htm (Accessed 6/1/2012).

(27) (NYT-Shoot Better) Schaffer Library of Drug Policy, *The Racial Roots of our Drug Laws,* Cites Dr. Edward H. Williams, *Negroe Cocaine 'Friends' Are a New Southern Menance,* Cites New York Times, Feb. 8, 1914, http://www. druglibrary.org/schaffer/library/histdrug.htm , (Accessed 6/1/2012).

(28) (Anti-China Laws) Schaffer Library of Drug Policy, *The Racial Roots of our Drug Laws,* http://www.druglibrary.org/schaffer/library/histdrug.htm (Accessed 6/1/2012).

(29) (Hillary Clinton) Whitney Eulich, *Pervasive Insecurity in Mexico: If this isn't 'terror, what is it?* Christian Science Monitor, December 3, 2011, http:// www.csmonitor.com/World/Americas/2011/1203/Pervasive-insecurity-in-Mexico-If-this-isn-t-terror-what-is (Accessed: 6/2/2012).

(30) (Iron River) Kevin Johnson, *ATF takes aim at deep 'Iron River of Guns,'* USA TODAY, March 18, 2009, http://www.usatoday.com/news/nation/2009-03-18-cartelguns_N.htm (Accessed 6/2/2012).

(31) (Gun Customers-Santa Claus) Associated Press, *Santa Poses with AK-47s at U.S. Gun Club,* The Guardian, November 30, 2011, http://www.guardian. co.uk/lifeandstyle/2011/nov/30/festive-firepower-santa-ak-47-us-gun-club (Accessed 6/2/2012).

(32) (March from Cuernavaca) Aljazerra (Americas), *Thousands March Against Mexico Drug Violence,* May 9, 2011, http://www.aljazeera.com/news/ americas/2011/05/201158191049940469.html (Accessed 6/3/2012).

(33) (Caravan for Peace) Ciara O'Rourke, statesman.com, *Group protests American drug policies at Capitol,* August 25, 2012 http://www.statesman. com/news/news/local/group-protests-american-drug-policies-at-capitol/ nRNmH/ (Accessed 11/10/2012).

(34) (Crime Rate Holland) Life Means Health, *Netherlands Closing Prisons Due to Plummeting Crime Rates,* http://www.lifemeanshealth.com/health-videos/health-politics/netherlands-closing-8-prisons-due-to-plummeting-crime-rates.html (Accessed 6/11/2012).

(35) (German Offer) Simon Sinhg, *The Zimmerman Telegram,* The Independent, http://simonsingh.net/media/articles/maths-and-science/the-zimmermann-telegram/ (Accessed 6/3/2012).

CHAPTER 3

(36) (Business Ranking) International Finance Corporation, The World Bank, *Doing Business- Economy Rankings,* http://www.doingbusiness.org/rankings (Accessed 6/3/2012).

(37) (3000 Maquiladoras) Matt Rosenberg , *Maquiladoras in Mexico,* About. com Geography, http://geography.about.com/od/urbaneconomicgeography/a/ maquiladoras.htm (Accessed 6/3/2012).

(38) (Employ 1 Million) Matt Rosenberg , *Maquiladoras in Mexico,* About. com Geography, http://geography.about.com/od/urbaneconomicgeography/a/ maquiladoras.htm (Accessed 6/3/2012).

(39) (Wages) Matt Rosenberg, *Maquiladoras in Mexico,* About.com Geography, http://geography.about.com/od/urbaneconomicgeography/a/ maquiladoras.htm (Accessed 6/3/2012).

(40) (Hours) Matt Rosenberg , *Maquiladoras in Mexico,* About.com Geography, http://geography.about.com/od/urbaneconomicgeography/a/maquiladoras. htm (Accessed 6/3/2012).

(41) (Maquiladora synergism) Jude Joffe-Block, Marketplace Business, *Arizona manufacturer sees Mexico as key to growth* October 29, 2012 http:// www.marketplace.org/topics/business/arizona-manufacturer-sees-mexico-key-growth (Accessed 11/10/2012).

(42) (GE) Charles Fishman, *The Insourcing Boom,* The Atlantic, December 2012, 45-52.

(43) (Aguilar- 1511) Jim Tuck, Mexconnect Online , *Jeronimo de Aguilar: the Marooned Priest who Speeded the Conquest,* http://www.mexconnect. com/articles/293-jeronimo-de-aguilar-the-marooned-priest-who-speeded-the-conquest , (Accessed 6/27/2012): William Hickling Prescott, *History of the Conquest of Mexico,* Vol 1 , (Hard Bentley, New Burlington Street, London), 247-249. http://books.google.com/books?id=YWg6AAAAcAA J&pg=PA247&lpg=PA247&dq=jeronimo+de+aguilar&source=bl&ots=-WqVXHW3B3&sig=dS91ygFG_AumSqSSnnQiz9t4T5U&hl=en&ei=u-_DTv--HOzhsQLG14GrCw&sa=X&oi=book_result&ct=result&resnum=13&ved=0CH 8Q6AEwDA#v=onepage&q=jeronimo%20de%20aguilar&f=false (Accessed: 6/3/2012).

(44) (20 Million) Arizona Daily Star, February 14, 2012, *Despite Drug Violence, 2011 was a Banner Year, Mexico Says,* http://azstarnet.com/news/ local/border/despite-drug-violence-was-banner-tourism-year-mexico-says/ article_cae1b32e-985d-5910-8f7a-1bb8c1be204e.html (Accessed 6/3/2012).

(45) (One Million Ex- Pats) Expat Forum. Com , *Expat Forum for Expats Living in Mexico,* http://www.expatforum.com/expats/mexico-expat-forum-expats-living-mexico/ (Accessed 6/4/2012).

(46) (Corruption Index) Worldwide Corruption Perceptions Ranking of Countries, *Transparency International (2011)*, Chart at Wikipedia, http:// en.wikipedia.org/wiki/Corruption_Perceptions_Index (Accessed 6/27/2012).

(47) (Police Wages)) AP Report: Yahoo News, *Many Mexican Police Still Get Low Wages,* http://news.yahoo.com/report-many-mexican-police-still-low-wages-185340813.html (Accessed 6/20/2012).

(48) (GDP) Marla Dickerson, *The Bite of Corruption,* Los Angeles Times, August 6, 2006, http://articles.latimes.com/2006/aug/06/business/fi-mordida6 (Accessed 6/4/2012).

(49) (1 out of 5) Marla Dickerson, *The Bite of Corruption,* Los Angeles Times, August 6, 2006, http://articles.latimes.com/2006/aug/06/business/fi-mordida6 (Accessed 6/4/2012).

(50) (Walmart) David Barstow, "Vast Mexico Bribery Case Hushed Up by Wal-Mart After Top- Level Struggle," *New York Times, Business Day,* April 21, 2012.

CHAPTER 4

(51) (Wonderful Old Tub) Tony Burton, *Did you know? Steamboats on Lake Chapala,* Mexconnect http://www.mexconnect.com/articles/3012-did-you-know-steamboats-on-lake-chapala (Accessed 12/5/2012).

CHAPTER 5

(52) (Bullring-40,000) Aboutmexico.net-your travel guide, *Bullfighting in Mexico,* http://www.aboutmexico.net/mexico/bullfighting.asp (Accessed11/14/2102).

(53) (Bullfighting Statistics) CAS International, *Bullfighting in Mexico,* http://www.cas-international.org/en/home/suffering-of-bulls-and-horses/bullfighting/mexico/ (Accessed 11/14/2012).

(54) (Water Bull Fights) CAS International. *Bullfighting in Mexico,*http://www.cas-international.org/en/home/suffering-of-bulls-and-horses/bullfighting/mexico/ (Accessed 12/5/2012).

(55) (San Felipe) Wikipedia, *Philip of Jesus,* http://en.wikipedia.org/wiki/Philip_of_Jesus (Accessed 11/14/2012).

CHAPTER 6

(56) (Chihuahuas) Orlando Sentinel, *Dogs of Mexico,* May 4, 2012 http://blogs.orlandosentinel.com/features_lifestyle_animal/2011/05/dogs-of-mexico-chihuahua-and-xoloitzcuintli-2.html (Accessed 11/14/2012).

(57) (Xolo) Orlando Sentinel, *Dogs of Mexico,* May 4, 2012 http://blogs.orlandosentinel.com/features_lifestyle_animal/2011/05/dogs-of-mexico-chihuahua-and-xoloitzcuintli-2.html (Accessed 11/14/2012).

CHAPTER 7

(58) (Number Sites Excavated) Wikipedia, *List of archaeological sites by country,* http://en.wikipedia.org/wiki/List_of_archaeological_sites_by_country#Mexico (Accessed 6/5/2012).

(59) (40,000 BCE) Michael C. Meyer, William L. Sherman & Susan M. Deeds, *The Course of Mexican History,* 7th edition (New York Oxford, Oxford University Press, 2003) 3.

(60) (9000 BCE-Melting Ice Stop Migration) Michael C. Meyer, William L.

Sherman & Susa M. Deeds, *The Course of Mexican History,* 7th edition (New York Oxford, Oxford University Press, 2003) 4.

(61) (10,000-8000 BCE Prehistoric Prey) Michael C. Meyer, William L. Sherman & Susan M. Deeds, *The Course of Mexican History,* 7th edition (New York Oxford, Oxford University Press, 2003) 4.

(62) (Tepexpan Man) Vincent H. Malmström, *Land of the Fifth Sun: Mexico in Space and Time*, http://www.dartmouth.edu/~izapa/LFS_Chapter%202.htm (Accessed 9/18/2012).

(63) (Disappear-7500 BCE) Michael C. Meyer, William L. Sherman & Susan M. Deeds, *The Course of Mexican History,* 7th edition (New York Oxford, Oxford University Press, 2003) 5.

(64) (Farming) Michael C. Meyer, William L. Sherman & Susan M. Deeds, *The Course of Mexican History,* 7th edition (New York Oxford, Oxford University Press, 2003) 5.

(65) (Corn-2000 BCE) Michael C. Meyer, William L. Sherman & Susan M. Deeds, *The Course of Mexican History,* 7th edition (New York Oxford, Oxford University Press, 2003) 5.

(66) (Hero Twins) Teaching the Myths, *Hero Twins,* http://www.mythweb.com/teachers/why/other/hero_twins.html (Accessed 6/27/2012); Wikipedia, *Maya Hero Twins* ,http://en.wikipedia.org/wiki/Maya_Hero_Twins (Accessed 6/27/2012); *The Hero Twins,* http://mayas.mrdonn.org/herotwins.html http://www.lindakreft.com/herotwins.html (Accessed 6/27/2012).

(67) (The Drunkards) Sacred Destinations, *Great Pyramid of Cholula, Puebla,* http://www.sacred-destinations.com/mexico/cholula-great-pyramid (Accessed 7/1/2012).

(68) (Hallucinogenic) Sacred Destinations, *Great Pyramid of Cholula, Puebla,* http://www.sacred-destinations.com/mexico/cholula-great-pyramid (Accessed 7/1/2012).

(69) (Across Atlantic-Pacific) (South Pacific/Iberia) Michael C. Meyer, William L. Sherman & Susan M. Deeds, *The Course of Mexican History,* 7th edition (New York Oxford, Oxford University Press, 2003) 4.

(70) (Fingerprints of Gods) Graham Hancock, *Fingerprints of the Gods,* Three Rivers Press, New York, NY) (Random House Inc., New York, Toronto, London, Sydney, Auckland, 1995).

(71) (UFO)) Forbidden History, *Mayan Astronaut,* https://www.forbiddenhistory.info/?q=node/100 (Accessed 12/14/2012).

CHAPTER 8

(72) (Manors-50 Rooms) Michael C. Meyer, William L. Sherman & Susan M. Deeds, *The Course of Mexican History,* 7th edition (New York Oxford, Oxford University Press, 2003) 83.

(73) (Population) Michael C. Meyer, William L. Sherman & Susan M. Deeds, *The Course of Mexican History,* 7th edition (New York Oxford, Oxford University Press, 2003) 82.

(74) (Gardens of World) PBS *Tenochitlan,* http://www.pbs.org/opb/

conquistadors/mexico/adventure1/pop-tenochtitlan.htm (Accessed 6/30/2012).

(75) (Seville)) Michael C. Meyer, William L. Sherman & Susan M. Deeds, *The Course of Mexican History,* 7th edition (New York Oxford, Oxford University Press, 2003) 82.

(76) (Montezuma-Palace) Michael C. Meyer, William L. Sherman & Susan M. Deeds, *The Course of Mexican History,* 7th edition (New York Oxford, Oxford University Press, 2003)85.

(77) ("White bearded men") Michael C. Meyer, William L. Sherman & Susan M. Deeds, *The Course of Mexican History,* 7th edition (New York Oxford, Oxford University Press, 2003) 87.

(78) (Nothing Remains) PBS *Tenochitlan,* http://www.pbs.org/opb/ conquistadors/mexico/adventure1/pop-tenochtitlan.htm (Accessed: 6/6/2012).

CHAPTER 9

(79) (Job Restrictions) Michael C. Meyer, William L. Sherman & Susan M. Deeds, *The Course of Mexican History,* 7th edition (New York Oxford, Oxford University Press, 2003), 193.

(80) (Mentally Inferior) Michael C. Meyer, William L. Sherman & Susan M. Deeds, *The Course of Mexican History,* 7th edition (New York Oxford, Oxford University Press, 2003), 196.

(81) (Santa Prisca-Borda) Michael C. Meyer, William L. Sherman & Susan M. Deeds, *The Course of Mexican History,* 7th edition (New York Oxford, Oxford University Press, 2003), 251.

CHAPTER 10

(82) (Burned at the Stake) Patricia Lopes Don, Journal of World History, *Franciscans, Indian Sorcerers, and the Inquisition in New Spain,* http://www. historycooperative.org/cgi-bin/justtop.cgi?act=justtop&url=http://www. historycooperative.org/journals
jwh/17.1/don.html (Accessed 7/6/2012).

CHAPTER 11

(83) (20 million at time of Conquest to One Million) U.S. Library of Congress http://countrystudies.us/mexico/53.htm (Accessed 7/14/2012)

(84) (Torturing Indians) Lambda Theta Phi, Fraternidad Latina, Inc., AO Chapter, http://www.umich.edu/~ltpao/conqui.html (Accessed 9/4/2012).

CHAPTER 12

(85) ("By the Grace of God") *Colonel John M. Chivington,* http://www. lastoftheindependents.com/chivington.html (Accessed 7/6/2012**).**

(86) ("Kill Them") *Colonel John M. Chivington,* http://www. lastoftheindependents.com/chivington.html (Accessed 7/6/2012).

(87) (Pope Paul) American Catholic, Saint of the Day December 9, 2012, *St. Juan Diego* http://www.americancatholic.org/Features/Saints/saint. aspx?id=1224 (Accessed 7/6/2012).

(88) (Bring Good News) American Catholic, Saint of the Day December 9,

2012, *St. Juan Diego* http://www.americancatholic.org/Features/Saints/saint. aspx?id=1224 (Accessed 7/6/2012).

CHAPTER 13

(89) (Marcos Identity) Teresa A. Meade, *A History of Modern Latin America:1800 to the Present,* Box 14.2 http://books.google.com/books? id=b 4oyihflfh0C&pg=PA328&lpg=PA328&dq=marcos+chiapas+rafael&source=bl&o ts=nsAK0GWWh9&sig=CLdBaDzc-FpJtZHyHjs4u20oChU&hl=en&ei=DVfFTuSSG MGnsQK9sb3BCw&sa=X&oi=book_result& ct=result&resnum=7&sqi=2&ved=0 CEgQ6AEwBg#v=onepage&q=marcos%20chiapas%20rafael&f=false (Accessed 7/6/2012).

(90) (Worst Record) Greg Campbell, Center for Advancement of Journalism and Zone Interactive, *The NAFTA War,* July 23-July 29, 1996, http://www. tc.umn.edu/~fayxx001/text/naftawar.html (Accessed 6/6/2012).

(91) (12% Land) Nation Master.com *Agriculture Statistics>Arable Land>....,* http://www.nationmaster.com/graph/agr_ara_lan_hec_percap-arable-land-hectares-per-capita (Accessed 7/6/2012).

(92) (Draw Straws) Paul Kingsnorth, *Zapatistas,* http://home.clara.net/ heureka/gaia/zapatistas.htm (Accessed 7/6/2012).

(93) (Death Toll) Nicholas Paul Higgins, *Understanding the Chiapas Rebellion: Modernist Visions and the Invisible Indian,* 91. http://books.google.com/books? id=s1DDVgxqiAMC&pg=PA91&lpg=PA91&dq=chiapas+death+toll+indians&sourc e=bl&ots=AUmeTzSFil&sig=vGN2znKXAQ5WITk0U6nRIaZpASI&hl=en&ei=OoTFT rumDe-62gXvt8yZBQ&sa=X&oi=book_result&ct=result&resnum=1&sqi=2&ved= 0CB0Q6AEwAA#v=onepage&q&f=false (Accessed 7/6/2012).

(94) (Harvard Conference) .* http://hir.harvard.edu/blog/jason-lakin/fifteen-years-after-the-zapatistas

CHAPTER 14

(95) (20,000+) Christopher Minster, *Mexican Independence – The Siege of Guanajuato,* About.com, Latin American History -- http://latinamericanhistory. about.com/od/latinamericaindependence/p/09guanajuato.htm (Accessed 12/12/2012).

CHAPTER 15

(96) (Santa Anna-Landholdings) Mexican History.org> *Santa Anna 1794-1876,* http://mexicanhistory.org/ (Accessed 7/6/2012) http://mexicanhistory.org/ santaanna.htm (Accessed6/7/2012).

(97) (The Leg) Roadside America. Com, *Captured Leg of Santa Anna,* http:// www.roadsideamerica.com/story/18808 (Accessed 7/6/2012).

(98) (Diaz-"So Far From God") Sandy Goodman, *"Poor Mexico, So Far from God, So Close to the United States,* March 1, 2009, Huffington, http://www. huffingtonpost.com/sandy-goodman/poor-mexico-so-far-from-g_b_170899. html (Accessed 7/6/2012).

(99) (Terrazas Wealth) Michael C. Meyer, William L. Sherman & Susan M.

Deeds, *The Course of Mexican History,* 7th edition (New York Oxford, Oxford University Press, 2003) 440.

(100) (On Their Own-Brenner) Anita Brenner, *The Wind That Swept Over Mexico,* (University of Texas Press, Austin) 30.

(101) (Unleashed a Tiger) Richard Cavendish, *The Ousting of Porfirio Diaz,* History Today, Volume 61:Issue 5, 2011, http://www.historytoday.com/richard-cavendish/ousting-porfirio-diaz (Accessed 7/6/2012).

(102) (Death Toll)) Christopher Minster, *The Mexican Revolution-Ten Years That Forged a Nation,* About.com, Latin American History http://latinamericanhistory.about.com/od/thehistoryofmexico/a/mexicanrevo.htm (Accessed 7/13/2012).

(103) (Population at Onset of Revolution) U.S. Library of Congress, *Mexico Population Statistics* http://countrystudies.us/mexico/53.htm (Accessed 7/13/201

CHAPTER 16

(104) (Obregon-Villa Assassination) The Storm that Swept Mexico, *Alvaro Obregón 1880-1928)* http://www.pbs.org/itvs/storm-that-swept-mexico/the-revolution/faces-revolution/alvaro-obregon/ (Accessed 7/12/2012).

(105) (Death Toll 90,000 Cristero)   James A. Haught, *Another Holy Horror: The Cristero War,* http://www.newwave.net/~haught/Cristero.htm (Accessed 6/13/2012).

(106) (Cardenas-"Order the Train") Michael C. Meyer, William L. Sherman & Susan M. Deeds, *The Course of Mexican History,* 7th edition (New York Oxford, Oxford University Press, 2003) 575,576: See also: Historical Text Archive, *Cardenas del Río (1895-1970) http://historicaltextarchive.com/ sections.php?action=read&artid=132* (Accessed 7/15/2012).

(107) (Cardenas on Prayer) Michael C. Meyer, William L. Sherman and Susan M. Deeds, *The Course of Mexican History*, 7th edition, New York Oxford, Oxford University Press, (2003) 578, wherein the authors cite Albert L. Michaels, *"The Modification of the Anti-Clerical Nationalism of the Mexican Revolution by General Lázaro Cárdenas and Its Relationship to the Church-State Détente in Mexico,* The Americas 26, (1969), 37.

(108) (49,000,000 acres) Michael C. Meyer, William L. Sherman and Susan M. Deeds, *The Course of Mexican History,* New York Oxford, Oxford University Press (2003), 576

(109) (Perfect Dicatorship) Paperback Swap, "List of Books by Mario Vargas Llosa" http://www.paperbackswap.com/Mario-Vargas-Llosa/author/ (Accessed 6/8/2012).

(110) (Llosa reference to "perfect dictatorship") Jo Tuckman, "Mexican Democracy Lost Years," *New York Times,* Sunday Review, June 24. 2012, 4.

(111) (Two Faced) *Mexico 1910-1989* http://www.google.com/url?sa=t&rct=j& q=&esrc=s&frm=1&source=web&cd=1&sqi=2&ved=0CEcQFjAA&url=http%3A% 2F%2Fwww.quia.com%2Ffiles%2Fquia%2Fusers%2Flisaperkins%2FSpanish3%2F

Mexico-5th&ei=IZUFULSmD8L_qwGZjqjbBQ&usg=AFQjCNE5TLi_0aX15Tzf8QFgd
xM1u_o0eQ&sig2=nXHIkhOkYZPKNF0ywt_MTg (Accessed 7/16/2012).
(112) (Tlatelolco Deaths) Michael C. Meyer, William L. Sherman and Susan M.
Deeds, *The Course of Mexican History*, New York Oxford, Oxford University
Press, (2003), p. 643
(113) (Government Estimate)) Michael C. Meyer, William L. Sherman
and Susan M. Deeds, *The Course of Mexican History*, 7th edition, New York
Oxford,Oxford University Press, (2003), p. 643
(114) (Colosio Death) Gregory Alan Gross, *Colosio's Death Still Vivid*, San
Diego Union Tribune, March 23, 2004, http://www.signonsandiego.com/
uniontrib/20040323/news_1m23greg.html (Accessed 6/8/2012) :See also:
Los Angeles Times ,*The Truth About Colosio's Murder? Credibility Gap Dogs
Mexican Government*, July 14, 1994, http://articles.latimes.com/1994-07-14/
local/me-15289_1_mexican-government (Accessed 6/8/2012).
(115) (Like a Dog) Chicago Tribune, *Jose Lopez Portillo, 83*,2/18/2004, http://
articles.chicagotribune.com/2004-02-18/news/0402180341_1_peso-mexican-
political-system-president-luis-echeverria (Accessed 6/8/2012).
(116) (Died for Sins) China Daily, *Mexico ex-President Lopez Portillo Dies,*
February 18, 2004, http://www.chinadaily.com.cn/english/doc/2004-02/18/
content_307156.htm (Accessed 7/15/2012).
(117) ($43 Million-Pemex) Michael C. Meyer, William L. Sherman and Susan
M. Deeds, *The Course of Mexican History,* 7th edition, New York Oxford,
Oxford University Press (2003), 658.
(118) (Chief) Michael C. Meyer, William L. Sherman and Susan M. Deeds, *The
Course of Mexican History,*7th edition, New York Oxford, Oxford University
Press (2003), 658.
(119) (600 million) Michael C. Meyer, William L. Sherman and Susan M.
Deeds, *The Course of Mexican History,* 7th edition, New York Oxford, Oxford
University Press (2003), 658.
(120) (108) (Citibank-Raúl) International Centre for Asset Recovery, *Raul
Salinas,* http://www.assetrecovery.org/kc/node/47b75cea-34a9-11de-9627-
1d322f879051.0;jsessionid=E6A31FEDDEF9713B6792CCE38E48D51B (Accessed
7/15/2012).
(121) (Safe Keeping) , Tim Weiner, *Swiss Give Mexico Bank Files Linked to
the Former President,* The New York Times, November 29, 2002, http://www.
nytimes.com/2002/11/29/world/swiss-give-mexico-bank-files-linked-to-the-
former-president.html?ref=raulsalinasdegortari   (Accessed 6/8/2012).
(122) (Repatriation) Basel Institute on Governance, International Centre
for Asset Recovery, *Raul Salinas,* http://www.assetrecovery.org/kc/
node/47b75cea-34a9-11de-9627-1d322f879051.0;jsessionid=E6A31FEDDEF971
3B6792CCE38E48D51B (Accessed 6/8 2012).
(123) (13th Largest Economy Per World Bank) Wikipedia, *Economy of Mexico,*
http://en.wikipedia.org/wiki/Economy_of_Mexico (Accessed 8/6/2012).
(124) (Trade Agreements) Angeles Villarreal, Congressional Research Service,

156

July 3, (2012) http://www.fas.org/sgp/crs/row/R40784.pdf, p,3 (Accessed 8/6/2012).

(125) (Hardest Working) Visa Journey.com, *Mexico is the hardest working country in world, study finds* http://www.visajourney.com/forums/topic/304936-mexico-is-the-hardest-working-country-in-the-world-study-finds/ (Accessed 8/6/2012).

(126) (10th Most Visited) United Nations World Trade Organization, *World Trade Rankings* http://en.wikipedia.org/wiki/World_Tourism_rankings (Accessed 8/6/2012)

CHAPTER 17

(127) (Octavio Paz-on Death) Octavio Paz, *The Labyrinth of Solitude*, Gore Press, (New York) 58.

CHAPTER 18

(128) (Izapalapa) Mysinchew, Jean de la Vaissiere, *Violence Blights Pope's Easter Peace Proposal,* Mysinchew, April 9, 2012, http://www.mysinchew.com/node/72264 (Accessed: 6/9/2012).

CHAPTER 19

(129) (Thomás Canabal) Time Magazine, *Milestones, April 19, 1943,* (http://www.time.com/time/magazine/article/0,9171,884892,00.html (Accessed 9/3/2012).

(130) (Rodrigo Alemán) Wikipedia, *Saints of Cristero War,* http://en.wikipedia.org/wiki/Saints_of_the_Cristero_War (Accessed 9/3/2012).

(131) (Bartolme Rebukes Conquistadors) *Bartolome de Las Casa, Missionary Priest, Defender of the Oppressed* http://elvis.rowan.edu/~kilroy/JEK/07/17.html (Accessed 7/15/201

(132) (Itrubide-300 Shot on Good Friday) NNDB -tracking the entire world, *Augustín de Itrubide,* http://www.nndb.com/people/511/000097220/ (Accessed 11/14/2012).

(133) (One Half of Land) Timothy Neeno, M.A. ,*The French Intervention in Mexico(1862-1867,* Military History on Line.com http://www.militaryhistoryonline.com/usmexicanwar/ (Accessed 7/15/2012).

(134) (Methodist Magazine) Francis Huston Wallace, M.A., D.D., *Mexico in Transition,* Methodist Magazine, Vol. 42, 117, http://books.google.com/books?id=58IQAAAAIAAJ&pg=PA117&lpg=PA117&dq=excesses+mexico+church+wealth&source=bl&ots=YxEEP9sumc&sig=1-bDRZ6ND_T5knmRWQOzKW-zISQ&hl=en&sa=X&ei=bxDxTvKQNIrKsQKpv8C0AQ&sqi=2&ved=0CC8Q6AEwBQ#v=onepage&q=excesses%20mexico%20church%20wealth&f=false (Accessed 7/15/2012).

(135) (Pope Lambasts Constitution-Tearing Souls)) Michael C. Meyer, William L. Sherman and Susan M. Deeds, *The Course of Mexican History,* 7th edition, New York Oxford, Oxford University Press (2003), 362.

(136) (Pope Lambasts Constitution-Public Thought)) Michael C. Meyer, William L. Sherman and Susan M. Deeds, *The Course of Mexican History,* 7th edition, New York Oxford, Oxford University Press (2003), 362.

(137) (Napoleon's Religion) adherents.com, *The Religious Affiliation of Military and Political Leader Napoleon Bonaparte,* http://www.adherents.com/people/pn/Napoleon.html (Accessed 11/14/2012).

(139) (Pope visit 2012) Rafael Azuk, World Socialist Web Site, *The Pope visit to Mexico deepens assault on secular state,* http://www.wsws.org/articles/2012/mar2012/papa-m21.shtml (Accessed 9/4/2012).

(138) (Nieto- Engagement Announcement) David Agren, Catholic News Service, *Church and state: In Mexico, new reality or pragmatic politics?* http://www.catholicnews.com/data/stories/cns/1002409.htm (Accessed 9/4/2012).

(140) (2nd Biggest Catholic Population) David M. Cheney, *Statistics by Country-By Catholic Population,* http://www.catholic-hierarchy.org/country/sc1.html (Accessed 6/13/2012).

(141) (Evils of Feminism) Hiding Under The Bed Is Not The Answer, *Feminism is Root of All Evil, The Catholic Church and Women's Rights in Mexico,* Sept 11, 2010 http://hidingunderthebedisnottheanswer.wordpress.com/tag/queretaro/ (Accessed 6/13/2012).

CHAPTER 20

(142) (Cost Tortillos) Ioan Grillo, "75,000 Protest Tortilla Prices in Mexico," *Washington Post (Associated Press,)* February 1, 2007, http://www.washingtonpost.com/wp-dyn/content/article/2007/01/31/AR2007013101343.html (Accessed 6/27/2012).

(143) (30%-Informal) Randall C. Archibo and Elizabeth Malkin, *Mexico Shifts Focus from Drug War to Economy,* New York Times, November 27, 2012.

(144) (Domingo's opera roles) Wikipedia, *Plácido Domingo,* http://en.wikipedia.org/wiki/Pl%C3%A1cido_Domingo (Accessed 6/5/2012).

(145) (Rosamorado Church) Jonathan Clark, *Mariachi Vargas de Tecalitlan,* chttp://mariachihistory.com/vargas.htm (Accessed 6/5/2012).

(146) (UNESCO) CNN Wire Staff, "Mexican mariachi music receives international recognition," *CNN Online, International Edition,* November 27, 2011, http://edition.cnn.com/2011/11/27/world/americas/mexico-mariachi-unesco/index.html (Accessed 6/5/2012).

(147) (Schools)) CNN Wire Staff, "Mexican mariachi music receives international recognition," *CNN Online, International Edition,* November 27, 2011, http://edition.cnn.com/2011/11/27/world/americas/mexico-mariachi-unesco/index.html (Accessed 6/5/2012).

(148) (Zumárranga) Atrium Musicologicum, *Music in Mexico* http://musicologicus.blogspot.com/2007/07/music-in-mexico.html (Accessed 6/28/2012).

CHAPTER 21

(149) (Bach-Distribution of Wealth) Fredrico Bach, *The Distribution of Wealth in Mexico,* Annals of the American Academy of Political and Social Science, Vol. 208, Mexico Today, (Mar., 1940), 70-77,

(150) (Expelled) Sarah L. Babb, *Managing Mexico: Economists from*

Nationalism to Neoliberalism, Princeton University Press, Princeton, New Jersey, Second Printing 2004, 55. http://books.google.com/books?id=dkoVC vyqoo0C&pg=PA55&lpg=PA55&dq=federico+bach&source=bl&ots=oznZFrdh 8h&sig=ZntkhYuQtNJsBPhZWWrDhkTtv0k&hl=en&sa=X&ei=EXWET4KMJcrFtg eEkKDUBw&ved=0CCMQ6AEwATgK#v=onepage&q=federico%20bach&f=false (Accessed 6/14/2012).

(151) (10%) Encyclopedia of the Nations, *Mexico-Poverty and Wealth,* http://www.nationsencyclopedia.com/economies/Americas/Mexico-POVERTY-AND-WEALTH.html (Accessed: 6/14/2012).

(152) (Forbes Richest Man) Kerry A Dolan, *Finding Mexico's Missing Billionaires* Forbes, March 30, 2011, Accessed: 6/114/2012 http://www.forbes.com/sites/kerryadolan/2011/03/30/finding-mexicos-missing-billionaires/ (Accessed 7/15/2012).

(153) (30%- middle class) Encyclopedia of the Nations, *Mexico-Poverty and Wealth,* http://www.nationsencyclopedia.com/economies/Americas/Mexico-POVERTY-AND-WEALTH.html (Accessed 7/15/2012).

(154) ($ 2 a Day) James William Smith, *Illegal Immigration in the United States,* Illegal Immigration Statistics, http://www.illegalimmigrationstatistics.org/tag/extreme-poverty/ (Accessed 7/15/2012).

(155) ($ 1 a Day-extreme poverty)) James William Smith, *Illegal Immigration in the United States,* Illegal Immigration Statistics, http://www.illegalimmigrationstatistics.org/tag/extreme-poverty/ (Accessed 7/15/2012).

(156) ($6600) CHOROS + ECHO, *The Eleven Richest Mexicans. By Way of Forbes Magazine,* http://www.chorusandecho.com/articles/view/the-worlds-richest-man-in-2011-and-other-mexican-billionaires_70934 (Accessed 9/4/2012).

(157) (Last Words) Jewish Virtual Library, *Leon Trotsky,* http://www.jewishvirtuallibrary.org/jsource/biography/Trotsky.html (Accessed 7/15/2012).

CHAPTER 22

(158) (40% PEMEX) El Universal Cartera, *Ingresos petroleros, el major aliado de Fox,* September 1, 2006 http://www2.eluniversal.com.mx/pls/impreso/noticia.html?id_nota=53687&tabla=finanzas (Accessed 6/12/2012).

CHAPTER 23

(159) (Right Wing News) Right Wing News, *ICE Agents Rebel Against Amnesty right wing news Through Policy,* http://rightwingnews.com/immigration/ice-agents-rebel-against-amnesty-through-policy/ (Accessed 6/9/.2012).

(160) (Environmental Problems) Betsy Hartmann, *The Greening of Hate: An Environmentalist's Essay,* Southern Poverty Law Center, July 2010 http://www.splcenter.org/greenwash-nativists-environmentalism-and-the-hypocrisy-of-hate/the-greening-of-hate-an-essay (Accessed 7/15/2012).

(161) (Snipers) Ryan Lenz, Intelligence Report ,(Southern Poverty Law Center), Fall 2012 Edition, *Death in the Desert,* 27

(162) (Minefield)) Ryan Lenz, Intelligence Report ,(Southern Poverty Law

Center), Fall 2012 Edition, *Death in the Desert,* 28

(163) (Net Zero) Sara Miller Llana, *Home Again In Mexico,* Christian Science Monitor Weekly, April 9, 2012, 27.

(164) (CSM Question) Lourdes Medrano, *Will 'Net Zero' Drain Essential US Labor Pool?* Christian Science Monitor Weekly, April 9 2012, 28.

(165) (Contribute Social Security) Global Action on Aging, *Illegal Immigrants Are Bolstering Social Security With Billions* http://www.globalaging.org/pension/us/socialsec/2005/illegal.htm (Accessed: 6/8/2012).

Acknowledgements

Special thanks to my wife, Mary, for allowing me the solitude of my basement desk for many hours at a crack over the last three years. Most important of her many contributions to this book was getting me to go to Mexico for the first time in 1976, and returning there with me countless times since then. We have chosen to celebrate our 50th wedding anniversary (which occurs in the year of publication) by having this book printed in the hopes that it will serve as a record for our four children (Paul, Brian, Jenny and Julie), their respective spouses, and our many grandchildren of the good times we had there and of the Mexican ventures we shared with them.. We also hope that this book will inspire its readers to appreciate this fascinating and often misunderstood country.

Special mention must be made of my sister, Nana, and her husband Dick, who for decades joined us on our Mexican adventures. They are veterans of untold hours of sitting on Mexican buses (which, in the early years, often meant sharing space with pigs and chickens); trudging through isolated ruins in thick jungles; being blown away by mariachi bands; and, in remote villages, suffering the indignity of cocktails without ice. Their children frequently were with us.

Some of the art works in the book are the creation of Enrique Velázquez; one is the creation of his wife, Belva. Both are well-known Mexican artists. Their e-mail address is belva@laguna.com.mx / and their web page is www.mymexicoart.com/. Their paintings can be viewed at their studio located at 16 de Septiembre # 7 in the lakeside village of Ajijic, Jalisco. A visit there is an essential part of the Lake Chapala experience. Their courtesy in allowing me to include some of their works in this book is greatly appreciated.

Some of the illustrations are the works of Kevin Willert, a talented artist of Manitowoc, Wisconsin. The photos on pages 32 and 44, and the photo on the back cover, belong to the author. Unless otherwise indicated, other images in the book (including the front cover) were procured by license from Dreamstime, http://www.dreamstime.com/.

Manitowoc Engraving, Inc. (www.manitowocprinting.com) is the printer of this book. Fred and Guy proved to be immensely helpful. I am grateful to them.

Dogs have always been a part of our lives, so having them with us in Mexico was never in question. I thank our many dogs for enduring thousands of miles of road travel over the space of many years and for making our ventures more fun.

161